Class and Character in Faulkner's South

February 6, 1977
Southern Short Story
Dr. Widmayer

Class and Character
in
Faulkner's South

MYRA JEHLEN

New York   **COLUMBIA UNIVERSITY PRESS**   *1976*

Library of Congress Cataloging in Publication Data

Jehlen, Myra.
   Class and character in Faulkner's South.

   Includes bibliographical references and index.
   1. Faulkner, William, 1897–1962—Criticism and
interpretation.   2. Southern States in literature.
I. Title.
PS3511.A86Z858   813'.5'2   76-3519
   ISBN 0-231-04011-3

Columbia University Press
New York   Guildford, Surrey

99699

For
Jessie

and for
Sonia, Albert, and Carl

Preface

Some will accuse this study of contentiousness and they will be right. The notion that an author's life and his understanding of history largely dictate the forms of his fictional universe seems unlikely to generate controversy. But its application to Faulkner has yielded controversy aplenty, with the result that I have frequently found myself insisting when I had meant only to suggest. Indeed, the problem of tone and language has been central throughout. I needed and did not have a neutral, analytical vocabulary to argue the basic critical relevance of the Southern class structure, or of Faulkner's views on race. For the difficulty in this country is that we have no traditional context for discussing, as an aspect of literature, the politics of race or class—or of literature.

Of course, there is a distinguished American criticism which does examine the relationship of works to their surrounding reality. The very discipline of American Studies itself sprang from the conviction that literature and history are mutually resonant. In certain basic ways, however, that tradition, with which I would want to associate nonetheless, does not solve the problems of method which arise in this essay. Many works in the field of American Studies deal, for instance, only with isolated linkages between a literary treatment and its materials. They thus stop short of constructing the cosmology that informs the writer's entire vision and which is implied by such linkages. Others, which are more structural in their approach, tend to abstract from the fictional world to some model of society *per se*, or even to some mythical realm beyond. Yoknapatawpha County, however, is neither a guide to Faulkner's home town nor an emblem of Civilization, not to say all Creation. Rather, Yoknapatawpha is a particular fictive totality, distinct in both its structural and its more accidental features, and at the same time Faulkner's projection of another particular totality, the American South. To analyze the relations between such totalities (that being my central concern, for reasons elaborated in the body of the essay) one needs a model internally cognizant of historical reality. Among such models, the Marxist one seems most relevant to dealing with the social and historical disposition of literature. But if Marxism is perhaps the place to start, it is at best only a beginning and can point the general direction. For if it is clear that we have been impeded in the development of our self-understanding because of the lack of a native Marxist tradition, it is also apparent that the one developed overseas is, as one would expect, organically tied to the distinct reality and consciousness of Europe. We need a critical method that is organically ours, and this book records one attempt, with all its gropings and false leads, to develop one.

If I have felt the lack of a supporting critical tradition, I have not wanted for personal support. It has been my privilege to have Henry Nash Smith as a rigorous teacher and a generous critic. Charles Sellers guided my earliest forays into Southern history. I would like to thank them, as well as Hugh Babinski, Sacvan Bercovitch, Joe Cady, Bell Chevigny, Carolyn Heilbrun, Fred Keener, Helene Moglen, Cicely Nichols, John Richetti, Carl Riskin, John Jacob Simon, and Alan Trachtenberg, who all in various ways contributed much-appreciated time, energy, and critical insight to this book. None of them, of course, is responsible for the outcome.

Contents

Class and Character in Faulkner's South

Introduction

William Faulkner was obsessed by history. Unlike many of his contemporaries for whom the exterior world had little reality and everything took place inside, he drew characters whose inner lives are essentially linings for selves tailored to unalterable social patterns. Others worried over protagonists lost in themselves, beyond time and place. His people's tragedy is that their interior world has been coopted by an external world they never made and apparently no one can ever unmake. In the chapters that follow, this historicity is my central concern. Faulkner's assumption that events and situations do attain an objective significance in their communal effect makes his work an ideal subject for a study of the relation of literature to social history. Closer in this respect to nineteenth-century realism than to his own more skeptical time, Faulkner wants to arrive at truth. If, as notably in *The Sound and the Fury,* he uses the techniques of subjectivity and multiple perception, it is because he senses that in our time knowing has become increasingly problematical; but knowledge for him has not. In other words, while he certainly doubts his characters' ability to uncover the truth, he does not really doubt that it exists somewhere. The problem for Faulkner is not that the world is only as we perceive it but that we may not be able to perceive it as it is.

His actual judgment of history, however, was as tormented as that of any modern, perhaps more so, since reality was for him inescapable. Where earlier American writing celebrated the journey out to an ever-promising frontier, Faulkner's "The Bear," for instance, beats a disillusioned retreat. Its hero Isaac McCaslin is a frustrated Natty Bumppo, a Daniel Boone who finds the wilderness already violated by some catastrophic teleology which has projected the past sins of his people onto all their descendants. In the American tradition,[1] he never seriously questions the propriety of man's conquest of nature—as long as the conquering civilization is worthy. But when he perceives that the virgin soil of Yoknapatawpha County has been plowed into a moral wasteland by its cavalier society, Isaac (Ike) withdraws from the then twice-fallen world.

On first joining the annual bear hunt which constitutes the story, he envisions a pastoral ritual, rebirth and initiation in the bosom of nature, an epiphany of sonorous abstract verities. These themselves, however, instead of easing his transcendence, direct Ike back to history, the history of his ancestors' betrayal. Perceiving himself mor-

[1] The European and the American versions of pastoralism are almost opposite concepts. The former values nature for itself, the latter primarily as a theater of human enterprise. Insofar as nature is inspiring for Americans, it is a challenge. Roman, English, and French pastoralists generally shared the opposite notion that man should abandon ambition and yield to the ways of nature. Americans do not as a rule yearn to return to the wilds; they are nostalgic for the opportunity to civilize.

ally disinherited, he understands that his internal landscape has been drawn less from nature than from civilization. His understanding of the situation, therefore, develops from subjectivity to a still personal but externally verifiable reality.

So Ike's earliest knowledge of the bear is wholly interior. Before his ever setting foot in the woods as a boy, Faulkner writes,

he had already inherited . . . without ever having seen it, the big old bear with one trap-ruined foot . . . the long legend of corn-cribs broken down and rifled, of shoats and grown pigs and even calves carried bodily into the woods and devoured and traps and deadfalls overthrown . . . a corridor of wreckage and destruction beginning before the boy was born, through which sped, not fast but rather with the ruthless and irresistible deliberation of a locomotive, the shaggy tremendous shape. It ran in his knowledge before he ever saw it. It loomed and towered in his dreams before he even saw the unaxed woods where it left its crooked print, shaggy, tremendous, red-eyed, not malevolent but just big, too big for the dogs which tried to bay it, for the horses which tried to ride it down, for the men and the bullets they fired into it; too big for the very country which was its constricting scope. It was as if the boy had already divined what his senses and intellect had not encompassed yet: that doomed wilderness whose edges were being constantly and punily gnawed at by men with ploughs and axes who feared it because it was wilderness, men myriad and nameless even to one another in the land where the old bear had earned a name, and through which ran not even a mortal beast, but an anchronism indomitable and invincible out of an old dead time, a phantom, epitome and apotheosis of the old wild life . . . the old bear, solitary, indomitable, and alone; widowered childless and absolved of mortality—old Priam reft of his old wife and outlived all his sons.[2]

Despite its interiority, we can readily see this description moving outward: Old Ben has become a myth by leaving real footprints in a real wilderness. Nothing in Ike's initial myth-making subjectivism finally exceeds the possibilities of realism. Balzac's most memorable characters are also exaggerated, becoming the embodiments of miserliness or of paternal love. But they and Old Ben really do exist in themselves, quite aside from the way they exist for other characters. That for a long time Ike's knowledge of the bear is incomplete does not render the bear incomplete; quite the contrary, it is the boy who will have to develop before he can comprehend its full, awesome reality. Ike's understanding expands outward, therefore, from intuition to senses to intellect, from the interior world to the light of common reason. What he has "divined" or dreamed, his senses will verify and his mind eventually ratify. And even if the imagination proves more perceptive than the senses or the intellect (the passage really claims only that it is quicker), they, all three, share the common task of apprehending the external world. What locates Faulkner's representation of the subjective in the tradition of Balzac rather than that of Joyce is the fact that the data the author provides for Ike's personal vision are meanings immanent in "the unaxed woods" and "the crooked print." In this sense the "apotheosis of the old wild life" which the bear has become is the opposite of an abstract archetype. When in

[2] "The Bear," *Go Down Moses*, originally published in 1942 (London, 1965), pp. 146–47. Page references will hereafter be given in the text.

the end Old Ben evokes Greek legend, it is Priam who is incarnated rather than the bear disembodied.

He is fully contained in time as well. The "anachronism," the "widowered childless" bear "absolved of mortality" has in fact taken over time as one drinks from the fountain of youth to prolong life indefinitely. "Bear" in the paragraph just cited is inevitably modified by "old" for, far from being ageless, the bear has been old abnormally long. Paradoxically, given its pre-historic status, that "shaggy tremendous" beast whose march across time is "a corridor of wreckage and destruction" that no one and nothing seems able to stop, embodies history itself. More precisely, it represents the way things become meaningful in Faulkner's fictive universe, through their historical manifestations. That the past which the bear embodies is not only terrifying but awesomely majestic and towers over a diminished present, sets Isaac McCaslin in the middle of a typically Faulknerian dilemma, the several versions of which form the subject of this essay. What I want to indicate at the start, however, is that these dilemmas are rooted in problems of history and society. Sooner or later, indeed, they inflict on Faulkner's characters a real social doom. For the terrible irony of the subjectively transcendent passage reproduced above is its implicit prophecy of objective death, first the old bear's, then Ike's and that of his whole civilization.

Isaac McCaslin's anti-*Bildungsroman*, then, is the story of a hunt in which all male McCaslins ritually participate. Each year the hunters set aside one day for the futile chase of an old bear. Thus far the pursuit has been conducted for its own sake; in fact the hunters have probably preferred not to succeed. But the good fight has eventually to end in a good kill, a fact that Ike has trouble grasping, for he seems to envision even the actual death of the bear as an ongoing, timeless event, an immortal moment of truth. The story counters these visions of transcendence by pointing to their contradiction in Ike's real experience. So the years are rushing by while Ike, "still a child, with three years then two years then one year yet before he could make one of the hunters," dreams with paradoxical impatience of the "immemorial flank" and the "timeless woods" (pp. 148, 152). It is an impossible, invalid dream. Although Isaac McCaslin seems still unaware when "his day came at last" (p. 147) that his own transcendence must ironically thrust the bear into history by marking the unique event of its death, we have known it from the start. Faulkner begins the story by recording an irreversible development. "There was a man and a dog too," he writes ominously, "this time" (p. 145).

Indeed even the ageless unsettled wilderness is first evoked in the context of time and society. "For six years now," Faulkner notes precisely, Ike had heard "the best of all talking. It was of the wilderness, the big woods, bigger and older than any recorded document" but here contained, recorded, and dated. Similarly, the hunters whose encounter with the wilderness is absolutely "the best game of all, the best of all breathing and for ever the best of all listening," can only grasp the experience through the "concrete trophies, the racked guns and the heads and skins" (p. 194), that their own actions have precipitated out of the eternal float.

In time Ike himself recognizes his inevitable involvement with history, however repellent he may find it. Realizing that his ancestors are inescapably his, he vows never to be theirs. It is not in the woods that he comes to this decision, but upon becoming a full member of the community at age twenty-one. The story thus completes a circular voyage from the hopeful quest for a new moral frontier back to the McCaslins of Yoknapatawpha County. In the fourth and longest section Ike concludes his travail "juxtaposed not against the wilderness but against the tamed land which was to have been his heritage" (p. 159).

It was as preparation for this heritage that he had joined the hunters. Not yet alienated from society, he is at the start also childishly unaware of the generic opposition of man and nature. At one with the cosmos, he sees the big woods as the stuff of poetry, an anthropomorphic nature co-extensive with his imagination. His first sight of the bear is described as a coming together, a fusion of the see-er and the seen that quite transcends object-subject distinctions. Abandoning gun, compass, and pretensions, Ike simply waits; then the bear "did not emerge, appear: it was just there, immobile, fixed in the green and windless noon's hot dappling . . ." It crosses a glade, "then it was gone. It didn't walk into the woods. It faded, sank back into the wilderness without motion as he had watched a fish, a huge old bass, sink back into the dark depths of its pool and vanish without even any movement of its fins" (p. 163). The passage ends deep in the boy's mind, for he has found in Old Ben and the ancient fish metaphors to mediate the tense but abstract oppositions between extreme youth and vast cosmic ages and between lone individuality and the community of all living things. The world is one.

But such metaphors are quite inadequate to mediate the social conflicts he must face if he is to inherit a plantation. These begin to emerge in the second part of the story when we learn more about the hunters and their motives. For example, the contrast between the camp retainers, Sam Fathers and Boon Hogganbeck, and their aristocratic employers raises issues not contained in the nature mythology of the first part. Sam Fathers is an old man of mixed black and Indian ancestry who lives in the woods the year round. Accurately named, he is the one who introduces Ike to the wilderness and who sets the scene for the boy's naïve attempt to merge into it. But Fathers then guides him past that stage by teaching him to be a hunter, untamed nature's worthy but inevitable opponent. It is also Sam Fathers who discovers and trains the dog Lion which will finally bring the bear to bay. For unlike the boy, the old man is naïve about neither wilderness nor civilization. A man in the mold of Natty Bumppo, by whom however society did much better, Sam Fathers might be viewed as a scout betrayed. His mission is to facilitate access to untamed nature. This calling he is practicing when he provides the hunters with Lion; but the civilization he serves aborts its new world. Although richly and inspiringly a father figure, he has *"no children, no people, none of his blood anywhere above earth that he would ever meet again"* (p. 163). So he dies along with the bear.

Of course the betrayal of Fathers is implicit from the beginning. The old man is also the antithesis of a scout, being an outcast. Even if Fathers were to meet any of his kind again, Ike slowly realizes, if any possibility of rightful descendance were to emerge, *"he could not have touched it, spoken to it, because for seventy years now he had had to be a negro"* (p. 163). This then is what the McCaslins and their kind have made of their new world: a preserve watched over by keepers themselves not considered fit to be free.

The schism that Ike now perceives between a natural ethic and the values of his civilization is radical and ultimately unbridgeable. However torn Cooper's Natty Bumppo was between his love of the undomesticated wilds and his political conservatism, he did in himself demonstrate a certain ethical harmony between nature and society. His betters honored him right along with the deer and the Indians. Had he wanted it, the Leatherstocking might ultimately have been admitted to the highest circles. But Sam Fathers can never be more than a servant, fortunate indeed to be no longer a slave. Indian and black among the County's wealthiest men, he represents both the expropriated and those who were themselves property. Ike's understanding of this marks his real initiation to manhood. Significantly, it is an understanding tuned less to race than to class. Out in the woods Ike discovers himself an aristocrat who, though more than incidentally white, is more importantly neither poor nor born of poor. He becomes class conscious; instead of ideals, he discovers ideology.

Now, of course all Yoknapatawphans are race conscious. But I suggest that this is not the most important distinction among them, that the underlying organizing principle in their social structure is class, more precisely the division between two classes of white society, the planters and the "rednecks." Exactly how Faulkner perceived this structure to work and its relation to the real South are the subjects of later chapters. To start, however, it is important to note that his recognition of class was nearly unique in the American canon. National dogma has had it from the beginning that there were no classes in America, or, given rapid social mobility, no need to thus identify anyone. But Faulkner does just that. His people are made of the stuff of class distinctions: they are planter or poor-white (some few in between and defined by that too) and become individual by being a variant of their type. Moreover their motivations and the plots of their stories most often have to do with maintaining, resenting, or refurbishing a social situation which is first of all class defined and only then regional or racial. The secondary importance of the latter may be surprising. But it should be recalled that the Yoknapatawpha saga is a white man's tale. White priorities prevail. For instance, slavery seems to Faulkner much more clearly evil than segregation because slavery generated a history of conflict with excluded lower-class whites. Beyond that it visited a Biblical curse upon the slave-owners. Segregation, on the other hand, he saw as having to do primarily with race, with lesser repercussions upon relations among whites and no clear divine import. It seemed to him correspondingly less serious.

Whatever can be said about Faulkner's relative unconcern with racism, it is his strong awareness of class that animates Yoknapatawpha County. Its energy is the greater, its forces the more complex for being generated internally out of the imbalance, the disharmonies within the social structure itself. The guilt of the cavaliers, for instance, is sharper because it is not diffused throughout a homogeneous community but thrown back at them from the often hostile interfaces of their society. Faulkner's South is homogeneous only in the sense of adding up to a coherent community; but that community itself is deeply rent and its parts in constant play. Characters define themselves out of stances and situations afforded by that play. The result is the living pulse of Yoknapatawpha which is Faulkner's major achievement. Where other American writers failed ultimately to grasp the tangibility of social context because, believing in the American myth of classlessness they could visualize society only as a universal and neutral setting, Faulkner treats society itself as his central character. His people can be realistic and yet, through their social identities, resonantly typological. On the contrary, the generality of characters in American fiction tends to the bizarre, the grotesque, the literally outlandish as its protagonists swell up to become their own universes. Faulkner's characters move about a well-defined society which contributes to their definition through a dialectic more characteristic of the European novel.

This dialectic operates in the juxtaposition of the growth of Ike's personality and his developing awareness of the social situation. As the fatal climax approaches, we learn more and more about its social rather than its archetypal significance. Thus when word spreads about the countryside that a dog has been found powerful enough to challenge Old Ben, people gather in camp who are not members of the hunt but have their own reasons for wanting him killed. They are "swampers," "gaunt, malaria-ridden men appearing from nowhere, who ran trap-lines for coons or perhaps farmed little patches of cotton and corn along the edge of the bottom, in clothes but little better than Sam Fathers' and nowhere near as good as Tennie's Jim's [a black McCaslin serf], with worn shotguns and rifles" (p. 169). With their arrival, the social universe surrounding the wilderness begins to press in from all sides as a context that erodes our sympathy for Ike's love of nature, and it shakes his conviction as well. We are not persuaded by the swampers, of course, nor do we develop much sense of them as people, but we begin to see that the issue is more complicated than it seemed at first. It may be only that our attention is becoming diverted from the wilderness to the society supplanting it, but we now begin to wonder whether it isn't within that society that the decisive problems lie rather than in some primordial conflict between man and nature.

The climax is reached in Part Three. The actual slaughter is performed by Boon Hogganbeck, "huntsman," as Ike puts it, to the princely Sam Fathers, but actually in the Yoknapatawpha hierarchy, a "redneck," "cracker," "poor white," or "white trash." Boon has "the mind of a child, the heart of a horse, and little hard shoe-button eyes without depth or meanness or generosity or viciousness or gentleness or anything else" (p. 173). With none of its graces, Boon is yet society's faithful henchman, the one who actually strikes the fatal blow, proving himself a perversion spawned not by nature but by civilization to do its dirty work. The civilization that devalued Sam Fathers and rendered him sterile now provides him with an assistant who is altogether debased. After the death of Old Ben, Ike will return to the woods to find Boon sitting under a tree fumbling to reassemble a gun all in pieces. Above him in the tree forty or fifty squirrels dart about chattering. At Ike's greeting, "he didn't even look up to see who it was. Still hammering he merely shouted back at the boy in a hoarse strangled voice: 'Get out of here! Dont touch [the squirrels]! Dont touch a one of them! They're mine!' " (p. 252). The wilderness has passed into private hands.

Part Four explains precisely what this means. The perverted uses of the land granted man "on condition of pity and humility and sufferance and endurance" (p. 197), are here documented for Ike in the account books of the Mc-Caslin plantation. The books provide his final disillusionment. From the abstract idealism of the nature myth at the story's beginning, Faulkner here comes down to figures, ledgers, an accretion of details that project the most tangible of realities. It is this documentary history of slavery and incest that brings Ike to renounce his heritage. Inspired by his experience in the wilderness, he will seek to atone for the sins of his ancestors through personal privation.[3]

But Faulkner does not really approve of this renunciation, despite its ample grounds. Ike's cousin is very persuasive when he argues that "the direct male descendant of him who . . . got the land no matter how . . . when it was a wilderness of wild beasts and wilder men, and cleared it, translated it into something to bequeath to his children for their ease and security and pride and to perpetuate his name and accomplishments" (p. 195), cannot now in good conscience relinquish it. The appeal is to familial responsibility and beyond that to a mature acceptance of history. For in his total withdrawal from social involvement, Ike has only flipped the coin of transcendence. On the first side had been the attempt to fuse with nature, something Sam Fathers and Old Ben himself had ruled invalid. What Ike cannot seem to do is to be a man among men, responsible to them and to their past. This may well be Faulkner's strongest moral imperative. Later, in Charles Mallison, he would create just such a character who, mor-

[3] Some have therefore seen Ike as a Christ figure. Faulkner's endorsement of the martyrdom is however so qualified that it seems more accurate to say that Ike is simply a man with a Christ complex.

ally superior to his compatriots, nonetheless remains among them to raise them. What this represents, of course, is the ethical implication of the sense of history which I have suggested is central to the Yoknapatawpha fiction. All through the novels young men find themselves in plights similar to McCaslin's having to take responsibility for a past they find to varying degrees repugnant. For all of them, as for Ike, a decisive moment equivalent in its historicity to the "tamed land" section of "The Bear" occurs to reveal the real substance of their burden.

They are engaged, in other words, in a quest for historical understanding. The Yoknapatawpha saga is a profoundly historical work in both content and form, something which Faulkner criticism has not generally recognized.[4] First by the French, whose abstractness is eas-

---

[4] I might cite here recent examples of such criticism focusing tellingly on Faulkner's most profoundly historical work. Lynn Gartrell Levins ("The Four Narrative Perspectives in *Absalom, Absalom!*" *PMLA*, Jan. 1970, pp. 35–47) does recognize the novel's historical dimension but essentially brushes it aside, arguing that Faulkner's real interest lies in the contrapuntal subjectivities of his four narrators. Levins thus projects Faulkner as a "formal pluralist" manipulating "separate literary modes" not in order to achieve a more complete single vision of the past but out of a neo-Jamesian fascination with the myriad possibilities of narrative perspective. In much the same vein, C. Hugh Holman ("*Absalom, Absalom!*: The Historian As Detective," *Sewanee Review,* Oct.–Dec. 1971, pp. 542–53) wonders "that Faulkner could have been as thoroughly modern as he was in *Absalom, Absalom!*, could have engaged with great success in the contemporary artistic gambit of how we know rather than what we know, and could still have used these startlingly new techniques to assert things about man that Aeschylus and Sophocles had stated. . . ." Here Faulkner's experimental modernism acquires content but of the most disengaged kind: if his writing is at once futuristic and classical, it bears only a functional, coincidental relationship to his own time and place. This amounts really to a critical consensus. Michael Millgate's *The Achievement of William Faulkner* (New York, 1966), perhaps the most respected study of the last de-

ier to explain, but subsequently even by Americans, Faulkner has been considered primarily an international modernist or an experimenter in literary form. Yet it seems almost perverse to treat a writer with his strong sense of history in abstraction from that concern.

The reason this has been done, I think, lies beyond Faulkner in the area of criticism itself. The various kinds of formalism ascendant in American letters have shared, if nothing else, the conviction that the literary work possesses an integrity altogether apart from its social setting. Certainly some relation, be it inspirational or defiant, to society is granted, but it is more of a diplomatic link than an organic one. In line with this view, one can always juxtapose literature and society and comment on how they interact, but it is too mechanical an enterprise, too external to either the work or the world, to be of much interest. I have attempted a different approach, one that treats the literary ediface of Faulkner's Yoknapatawpha and the historically recognizable evolution of his Mississippi as parts of the same universe representing different modes of knowing and talking about it. It is clear that absolute objectivity is no more available than its antithesis. One way to view creative thinking, therefore, is as vision about the world keyed by a principle of interpretation. When it addresses it-

---

cade, warns us against mistaking Faulkner's means for his ends by concentrating on his involvement with Southern and American history. But the dichotomy which Millgate tacitly assumes between the historical and the universally significant is in itself profoundly alien to Faulkner's view of history as the very concretion of the transcendentally universal. The large meanings one reads in his stories need neither escape nor even transcend history since they illuminate it. It is history that he places in perspective and not perspective accidentally in history, his literary techniques being organically one with the meanings they uncover.

self to how people live in groups, this organizing principle amounts to an ideological syntax.[5] The usefulness of this syntax in governing the author's language manifests itself in two ways: with relation to the range and scope of the fictive realm, but also to the providing of materials from which it is constructed. As chapter 2 suggests, the difference in literary quality between *Absalom, Absalom!* and *The Unvanquished* grows largely out of the difference in the social stuff which opposite ideological approaches furnished to their creation. One approach made available to Faulkner the full complexity of Southern experience, the other denied it. In both cases the key to the work and, precisely, to the wholeness of its special imagined universe, lies in its ideology.

One last word concerning the methodology of this essay. I am quite aware that my analysis can become excessively schematic. That Faulkner's writing is distinguished above all by its rich complexity only makes this the more apparent. Rather than attempt to evoke that complexity, however (something done by others in abundance), I have constructed a kind of prism through which the lush Yoknapatawpha landscape can be seen to contain an inherent order. Viewing this order need no more impede one's appreciation of Faulkner's extraordinary range than a real prism dims the sun. Moreover, since my intent is in fact to propose a schematic model, I have thought it on balance

---

[5] This ideological syntax has little in common with the concept of a free-floating *Weltanshauung*. I mean something both more structured and more dynamic. More structured in the sense that it comprises an organic set of assumptions about the way social reality is constructed deep down and as a totality; more dynamic because this set of assumptions is the product of dialectic encounters between an inherently ordered world and an individual who is part of that world but also tries to understand it.

more useful and appropriate to the method to choose, where there was choice, the argument's sharper edge. But criticism begins in a dialogue with work and author, and it should issue in dialogue as well. *Class and Character in Faulkner's South* is written in that spirit.

1

Among Black and Savage Stars

The land's living symbol—a formal group of ritual almost mystic significance identical and monotonous as milestones tying the county's ultimate rim as milestones would: the beast the plow and the man integrated in one foundationed into the frozen wave of their furrow tremendous with effort yet at the same time vacant of progress, ponderable immovable and immobile like groups of wrestling statuary set against the land's immensity.[1]

The pastoral backwaters of Mississippi seem not to have afforded Faulkner much peace. The stories and novels of the Yoknapatawpha saga are tense with extreme, unresolvable contradictions which led one critic to suggest that the works indeed constitute a "quest for failure."[2] A major

[1] William Faulkner, *Intruder in the Dust* (New York, 1948), p. 147.
[2] Walter J. Slatoff, *Quest for Failure* (Ithaca, N.Y., 1960). Slatoff notes the preponderance of oxymorons in Faulkner's style and suggests that these express the author's reluctance to resolve fictional conflicts.

contention of this essay is that the tensions and disso-
nances in Faulkner's writing were neither temperamental
nor linguistic in origin [3] but expressed the author's profoundly discordant view of Southern life.[4]

The passage cited above captures the paradoxically violent paralysis pervading Yoknapatawpha, and the farming
image is altogether appropriate because the agrarian issue
was the central one in Faulkner's indecision. For in defin-

---

[3] Slatoff attributes Faulkner's preference for irresolution to his "temperament." See "The Edge of Order: The Pattern of Faulkner's Rhetoric,"
reprinted in *William Faulkner; Three Decades of Criticism,* ed. Frederick J.
Hoffman and Olga W. Vickery (East Lansing, Mich., 1960), pp. 197–98. The
linguistic origin has been proposed by James L. Guetti in his book,
Limits of Metaphor: A Study of Melville, Conrad and Faulkner (Ithaca,
N.Y., 1967). Guetti argues that for Melville, Conrad, and Faulkner "the
problem of order" is "linguistic" rather than "ideological" (p. 11). The
"narrative difficulty" for these writers "is that of using language in such a
way as to prevent one's recognition of the arbitrariness and exclusiveness
of composed linguistic systems" (p. 4). But while this interpretation is
highly resonant for us, concerned as we are with both the validity and
viability of language, it does not seem to me applicable to Melville or
Faulkner whose efforts are rather focused on the tensions not "within language" but "between language and a non-linguistic reality" (p. 4).

[4] Cleanth Brooks, in an important study, *The Yoknapatawpha Country*
(New Haven, Conn., 1963), has as a central thesis a view of the South and
of Faulkner's perception of it which is directly opposed to the one I develop here. Brooks sums it up this way: "Most of all, [the Yoknapatawpha]
society is bound together by unspoken assumptions—that is to say, it is a
true community" (p. 368). As is already evident, I do not think this society
or its real-life model is much united, nor do I think that Faulkner thought
it was, at least while he was writing his most important works. There Yoknapatawpha and the South appear deeply rent by moral and ideological
antagonisms rooted in a discordant class structure. I can see little evidence for Brooks's hopeful conclusion that "even lack of purpose and
value take on special meaning when brought into Faulkner's world, for its
very disorders are eloquent of the possibilities of order. . . ." (p. 368).
Faulkner's seems to me on the contrary one of the most troubled and
unresolved visions in America's troubled and unresolved literature.

ing his ideal of rural life, he was torn between two forms of agrarianism, both native to his region, but so opposed in their values and social implications that their partisans were joined in warfare long before the Civil War. Although the legendary cavalier has represented the South nationally, the region always had many more farmers than leisured planters. The struggle between these two agrarian groups roughly constitutes Southern political history, until the year 1939 anyway, and therefore through Faulkner's most impressionable and productive years. Each group rightly viewed the other as a threat to its survival. Sensitized by their dread of slave insurrections, the planters at times feared a redneck revolution. Of course the rednecks did seek a revolution of sorts or, at any rate, redistribution of the land and an equal share in political power.

The myths in which the antagonists embodied their aspirations became essential weapons in their fight.[5] The farmers cast themselves as Jeffersonian yeomen, upright tillers of the soil, the salt of the American earth.[6] The planters invoked classical ideas of order to legitimize their feudal system and argued that only a leisure class could attain the esthetic and ethical excellence to forward the course of civilization.[7] The common folk replied that their

[5] In *Origins of the New South, 1877–1913, A History of the South,* Vol. ıx (Louisiana State Univ. Press and the Little Field Fund for Southern History of the Univ. of Texas, 1951), C. Vann Woodward describes the way the Populists appealed to the Jeffersonian myth to validate their efforts and concludes that the myth was crucial to their success.

[6] The figure of the American yeoman has been analyzed in a number of works, chief of which is Henry Nash Smith's *Virgin Land, The American West as Symbol and Myth* (New York, 1961).

[7] The Southern cavalier and his values are exhaustively described in William R. Taylor, *Cavalier and Yankee. The Old South and the National Character (Garden City, N.Y., 1963).*

righteous labor fed the spirit as well as the body. They were translating into the Southern vernacular the words of Hector St. John de Crèvecœur who had written over a century earlier that "the salubrious effluvia of the earth animate our spirits, and serve to inspire us." [8] Most of Faulkner's contemporaries in the South seem to have aligned themselves with one or the other side. The majority of those involved in the Southern renascence of the twenties and thirties [9] agreed with Stark Young of Mississippi that "in talking about Southern characteristics we are talking largely of a certain life in the Old South, a life founded on land and the ownership of slaves." They defined agriculture as "a form of labor that is pursued with intelligence and leisure." [10] On the other hand, there were those like Ben Robertson who proudly claimed that his North Carolina ancestors were "plain people, . . . hickory-nut homespun Southerners." "Like Jefferson," he explained, "we believe in a country of small farms, with every family independent. . . . We believe in hard day labor. . . . All that eat should sweat." [11] Faulkner was heir to both of these viewpoints and unable fully to approve either one.

Since this ambivalence is a central theme of the essay, I should state at the outset that, far from regretting or condemning it, I consider it the source of Faulkner's literary

[8] J. Hector St. John de Crèvecœur, *Letters from an American Farmer* (New York, 1957), p. 12. The *Letters* first appeared in 1782.

[9] I refer, for example, to many of the group who cooperated in writing *I'll Take My Stand, The South and the Agrarian Tradition* (New York, 1962): Donald Davidson, Lyle H. Lanier, Stark Young, Allen Tate, Andrew Nelson Lytle, F. L. Owsley, and John Crowe Ransom. The book, a collection of essays, appeared in 1930.

[10] *I'll Take My Stand*, p. xxix.

[11] Ben Robertson, *Red Hills and Cotton, An Upcountry Memory* (New York, 1942), p. 98.

greatness. In fact one might speculate that some such ambivalence is the source of all artistic achievement. Resolution and clarity may yield theory, but the practice of literature seems to require another inspiration altogether. The well-known story of Faulkner's ranking of contemporary writers, giving first place to those who attempted the most and proved it by not succeeding, may well express his sense that the resolution of problems can be paradoxically fatal to the work, while the unceasing drive to resolve them is the very dynamic of creation. Something like this, at any rate, inspired Faulkner, whose own ambivalence was surely one of the most creative any writer ever suffered from.

In principle he seems to have endorsed Jeffersonian values. Yet it is clear from the preponderance in his major fiction of lords over peasants, that he felt the lords were the crux of the matter, the ones upon whom everything depended and foundered. This deference to a class whose way of life he considered ethically unwholesome, and the inverse, his inability to identify with the farmers, who, however abjectly, wore the yeoman's mantle, largely inspired the author's tragic vision of the South.[12] He did attempt a more hopeful vision focused on such modified aristocrats as Gavin Stevens and his nephew Charles Mallison. The scion of an old plantation family and himself committed to an abstract agrarianism which reveres the land however it is used, Stevens is the county's impartial district attorney, thus, it would seem, escaping the limitations in Faulkner's mind of either agrarian party. Gavin even makes

[12] Especially after his speech of acceptance for the Nobel Prize Faulkner himself and his critics tended to stress his affirmations and optimism. But these take the form mostly of abstract pieties while his "nays" are concretely realized in his best works such as *The Sound and the Fury* and *Absalom, Absalom!*

gestures toward reconciling the lords and the peasants in regard to such matters as educational and linguistic differences, for, unspoiled by the most enviable credentials,[13] he loves nothing better than long laconic afternoons on the porch of the general store, savoring a colloquial "chaw" with the locals. But whether King's English or vernacular, all Stevens can finally offer are words, an urbane commentary which views the passing of the Old South as one of life's cosmic ironies. Faulkner himself seems to have been less disposed to be philosophical about it; his sorrow is more rebellious than Gavin's and becomes at times a frantic search for an explanation—which, however, when it emerged in his work proved unacceptable because it implied that the major guilt was the planters'.

His emotional, perhaps "esthetic," bias in favor of aristocrats not only kept Faulkner in turmoil over the meaning of the Southern rural tradition, but also caused him some literary difficulties. These appear especially in the very uneven Snopes trilogy, *The Hamlet, The Town,* and *The Mansion,* written relatively late in Faulkner's career and thus coinciding with a slight but artistically significant drift to the political right. By this I refer, of course, not to a declared shift from left to right—the very small distance he moved would be of scant interest to a practical politician—but to something more subtle having to do with the way he interpreted his material and with the degree of critical independence he maintained toward his subject. In discussing Faulkner's political thinking, I mean simply his so-

[13] Stevens holds degrees from Harvard and Heidelberg universities. By "critical independence" I mean a stance resembling that of Georg Lukacs' definition of the critical realist writer, in *Studies in European Realism* and *Realism in Our Time.*

cial judgment—most significantly, the social categories in which he grouped individuals and by which their uniqueness was, for him, more or less attenuated. This aspect of his political views is especially important because it contributed to the definition of his characters. Faulkner's class bias was thus directly involved in the formal, most purely "artistic" aspects of his writing. The aristocrat Bayard Sartoris and the redneck Flem Snopes, for example, originate as characters in a political viewpoint which is in this respect indistinguishable from literary vision. And the fact that Sartoris is in formal terms a three-dimensional character and Flem Snopes an allegorical cipher [14] is not so much a matter of artistic choice as of social judgment. Indeed, that Faulkner regarded the upper class less critically toward the end of his career is here first of literary and only secondly of biographical or political interest.[15]

At any rate, during the years 1925 to 1940, when his major works appeared (*Sartoris, The Sound and the Fury, Light in August, Absalom, Absalom!,* most of the stories in *Go Down Moses,* and much of *The Hamlet*), Faulkner's attitude toward Southern society remained essentially constant, defined uneasily by the indecision described earlier. Under its influence he began with *Sartoris* (1929) an exploration of plantation history which reached an artistic and intellectual culmination in *Absalom, Absalom!* (1936).

Sartoris, Absalom, Absalom! and the other major cavalier novel, *The Sound and the Fury,* share a central plot, the story of a young man who wishes he could look toward the

[14] See chapter 5 for a discussion of this point.
[15] The same applies to Faulkner's racism as a factor in the literary analysis of chapters 3 and 4.

future but who is self-destructively driven to recall a fatal
post. In *Sartoris,* Bayard tries to reconstruct the death of his
brother while wondering all the time whether he himself
has not also been killed, "trying to remember, feel, a bullet
going into his own body that might have slain him at the
same instant." [16] Quentin Compson recalls the past in *The
Sound and the Fury* while in the process of committing
suicide, simultaneously succeeding in both. In *Absalom,
Absalom!* Quentin dies vicariously. The development of
this "recalling plot" through the Yoknapatawpha plantation
novels charts the general progress of Faulkner's early literary thinking.

In fact the recalling plot appears in Faulkner's first
novel, *Soldiers' Pay,* thus providing a sort of prehistory to
the Yoknapatawpha saga which is not to begin really until
four years later with *Sartoris.* In *Soldiers' Pay* the archetypal
seeker after the past is a critically wounded World War I
veteran returned to Georgia in a walking coma, and alive to
only one insistent need, to remember the circumstances of
his fatal wound. The structure of the later situation is already clear here: a man lives only to discover the cause of
his death and dies when he succeeds. Why the hero, Donald Mahon, should be so concerned with the exact manner
in which he was hit, and, more to the point, why we should
care how it all happened when the fatal moment seems to
have no further significance, is never explained. As a result, the puzzling lack of content in Donald Mahon's quest
calls attention to its empty form and, looking forward, to
the content of the *Sartoris* and later quests. The Bayard of
Sartoris is a veteran like Mahon trying to reconstruct a
World War I battle. The War itself seems altogether in-

[16] William Faulkner, *Sartoris* (New York, 1961), p. 272.

cidental to both stories, which leaves *in vacuo* the plot of *Soldiers' Pay*. But *Sartoris* begins to explain why the circumstances of a past fatal moment should become the goal of an obsessive search whose success is also fatal.

Briefly, the explanation lies in Bayard's regional and class identity, in his status as a descendant of the Southern plantation aristocracy who must try to understand himself through his heritage even though what he finally grasps is the awful fact of his own doom. Retrospectively, it becomes evident that this was obscurely also the motive of the recalling plot in *Soldiers' Pay* where the novice author tried to adapt it to the fashionable theme of the First World War.[17] What Donald Mahon finally remembers is described in these puzzling terms: "And suddenly he . . . was passing . . . again into a day that had long passed, that had already been spent by those who lived and wept and died, and so remembering it, this day was his alone: the one trophy he had reft from Time and Space."[18] What have "those who lived and wept and died" to do with the flight in which he was trapped by German planes? How is the act of remembering intrinsically courageous? And why is it significant that the memory of an event which occurred when he was anyway alone, now be "his alone"? The point is, of course, that even then Faulkner was not thinking of an air battle at all but, however obscurely, of the fall of the cavalier South. Later Bayard Sartoris and Quentin Compson would reconstruct that fall with bitter courage and the sense of being doomed survivors and victims of a history

---

[17] *Mosquitoes* (1927), which followed *Soldiers' Pay* (1926), is an even more fashionable book about urban sophisticates adrift in New Orleans. Faulkner was still groping his way to Yoknapatawpha.

[18] William Faulkner, *Soldiers' Pay* (New York, 1961), pp. 202–03.

which is paradoxically their only valued possession. But the wounded soldier here recalling a "day that had long passed" already foretells later, more meaningful quests.

Thus Faulkner's first idea for a fictional situation, the story he wanted to write when he began writing, was about a man for whom the past is all meaningful, and means death. *Soldiers' Pay* defines the form of this story in an allegory of moot significance with only the trappings of intense drama. Then *Sartoris,* the first of the Yoknapatawpha stories, rationalizes the plot of *Soldiers' Pay* by re-placing it in the Southern context from which it originated, though probably subconsciously.

Sartoris really tells the same story as its predecessor but with one major difference, for the emergence of Faulkner's historical concerns, now no longer rendered in psychological abstractions but directly and in context, resulted in an important modification of the recalling plot: the fatally wounded man is not Bayard himself but his brother. Without at all lightening or loosening the fate embodied in the recalled death-blow, the differentiation between the actual direct victim and his chronicler transforms a private into a social catastrophe, or a subjective, internal experience into history. Faulkner doubles his victims very carefully, elaborately stressing the closeness of the twin brothers so as not to locate Bayard too far from that fatal moment. The two youths seem sometimes to blend into one. When, for example, their aunt finds a painting of Johnny (the now dead twin) at the age of eight but cannot find Bayard's, it is as if the two boys had shared a single childhood. The impression is later strengthened when Johnny's widow looks at the picture of her husband and mistakes it for one of Bayard. In fact no one seems to remember Bayard's boyhood although Johnny's is constantly referred to, again as if Bayard had grown out of the child Johnny. And Bayard himself, wondering all the time whether he is not already dead, probes his brother's life for self-knowledge as if it were his own.

The sense of a dual identity is thus finally evoked wherein a dead man remains alive to observe and evaluate his own death, providing Faulkner with a way to describe both a timeless cataclysm (as it were, a mythical event) and its historical impact. In *Soldiers' Pay*, Donald Mahon is specifically outside history and reality, existing in the extension of a single instant which for him and the novel has exploded time and ended all processes. But Bayard, in trying to recreate a similar instant in the life of his brother, stands firmly within history, engaged in trying to understand how a particular moment can destroy the viability of all succeeding moments, how an event in history can negate all further historical processes or, rather, doom them to its own destruction. This changed plot is most fully elaborated in *Absalom, Absalom!* but *Sartoris* already contains its essential structure. The saga of Yoknapatawpha civilization thus opens with a sort of Wagnerian dirge or a decline-and-fall which will culminate, in the classical mode, with the barbarian invasion of the Snopeses. Or, in the terms of the novel's own imagery, "Sartoris" bespeaks a feudal empire which falls prey to Southern cousins of the Connecticut Yankee.

But if he hates Snopes commercialism, Faulkner also blames the improvidence of Southern knights. Their lost splendor, he complains, always shone brightest in fatal encounters, "for there is death in the sound of (Sartoris) and a glamorous fatality like silver pennons downrushing at sunset or a dying fall of horns along the road to Roncevaux." [19] Or, in the plain style of the twins' aunt, "it's in the blood. Savages, every one of 'em. No earthly use to anybody!" (p. 37). What she means is that Bayard and Johnny recall an aristocratic Southern character often featured in plantation fiction—the reckless if gallant planter, who dissipates his lands in gambling and drink, withal retaining his charm and poise. The type is familiar and, as we will see, the critique rather superficial. But it is surprising to recognize here in a 1929 work a literary convention dating back to before the Civil War and elsewhere discarded with the Confederacy. For Faulkner's contemporaries who dealt with the cavalier as such, like Stark Young, wrote in a different vein perhaps best represented by Thomas Nelson Page who smiled through his tears at the memory of the pure, halcyon days of slavery.

In fact, *Sartoris* does begin a little in that mode with the ghost of the twins' great-grandfather John dominating the first two pages and defining "Sartoris" in his own glamorous image, so that it seems for a while as if Faulkner intended us to see John Sartoris representing the greatness of the South squandered by its unworthy suicidal heirs. But on the third page the giant out of the past fades back to reappear only episodically, as the story focuses instead on the troubled great-grandsons who inform the family name with equivocal virtue.

What is surprising about this shift in focus is that it represents abandoning the aging post-War cavalier myth only to resume an even older, indeed pre-War debate which had attended the formation of the myth. William R. Taylor has shown that before the War, even writers fully commit-

[19] *Sartoris*, p. 254. Page references will hereafter be given in the text.

ted to the plantation system constituted a kind of loyal opposition and criticized it more often than they glorified it. They were especially concerned with the effect of autocratic power and of idleness on the character of the planter: precisely the aspect of feudalism that also most disturbed the Jeffersonian Faulkner. (One of these writers, James K. Paulding, even attempted to reconcile yeoman values with plantation life by depicting in *Westward Ho!* a sober, hard-working planter who participated materially in that labor process which mythically sanctifies the farmer.) Faulkner entered the discussion on this level and explored in *Sartoris* the viability of the cavalier stance as it had functioned in the past and as Bayard and Johnny inherited it.

Early in the novel their aunt, Miss Jenny, illustrates the Sartoris character in a legend about an ancestral Bayard killed in the War. She tells of dashing young men led by Jeb Stuart, "his plumed hat in his hand, and his long tawny locks tossing to the rhythm of his steed . . . like gallant flames smoking with the wild and self-consuming splendor of his daring" (p. 33). One day they sally forth in search of coffee, galloping between "vernal palisades" in a "jocund forest" whose silence they shatter with the "importunate alarms" of their bugles. (Note the feudal idiom of her tale.) At length they ride into the midst of a Yankee encampment, snatch a coffeepot, and canter away taking a hostage. When the kidnapped Yankee taunts them for their failure to capture some treasured anchovies as well, Bayard returns and is shot in the back by an irate cook. All this "in a spirit of pure fun: neither Jeb Stuart nor Bayard Sartoris, as their actions clearly showed, had any political convictions involved at all." With evident irony Faulkner reports that Miss Jenny views this incident as a "gallant and finely tragical focal point to which the history of the race has been raised from out the old miasmic swamps of spiritual sloth by two angels valiantly fallen and strayed, altering the course of human events and purging the souls of men" (p. 33).

As for himself, here at the beginning of *Sartoris*, Faulkner considers Bayard's and Stuart's exploit as merely "a hare-brained prank of two heedless and reckless boys wild with their own youth" (p. 33). But however qualified it may be by humorous affection for the romantic lads, this condemnation of them is significant and constitutes a first step toward the radical critique of *Absalom, Absalom!* Perhaps comparison with the contemporary cavalier novel *So Red the Rose* can highlight the importance of Faulkner's still minimal disaffiliation.

Stark Young's Duncan Bedford is the ostensible double of the Confederate Bayard Sartoris. His mother fondly recalls his many pranks: just for fun he once fired the corn-stacks on the campus of the University of Virginia, admitted it but proudly refused to apologize, sending the president of the University into apoplexy. He loves his horses better than anyone or anything, and has "knocked the head off" a churlish farmer who refused him free oats. But his most interesting exploit with relation to Bayard is his participation in the same legendary raid on the Yankee stores. In this version hams rather than coffee are the prize, but the real difference is that Duncan survives triumphantly. For despite his attitude toward the War—"as if the cavaliers were on a big hunt or running horseraces"—Duncan is not at all inadequate to the serious needs of the South and the War. A miniature his proud mother treasures shows him "at first sight to be in a fury of some sort; the fury then, when you glanced at him again, spread into impulsive pride, and from that suddenly it became the most astonishing air of generous youth and elegance combined." [20] Thus captured in living color, Duncan is the South's best hope, recklessly dashing, like Jeb Stuart, but as sound and stalwart as Robert E. Lee. The difference between Duncan and Bayard is crucial. "Jeb Stuart wins victories," remarks a shrewd friend of Mrs. Bedford's. "Otherwise I daresay he would seem reckless." [21] But the foolhardy Sartorises win no victories and by the end of the book Faulkner condemns even their romance as "humorless and fustian vainglory." [22]

Which is not to say that Faulkner was here rejecting the aristocratic culture. However disenchanted he appears at the end of *Sartoris*, it is only the style of plantation life that he has challenged and not its substance. Moreover, this style seems to be a mysteriously inherent quality that defines the Sartoris way of life independently of their social context. Perhaps after all, the novel allows us to think, it *is* "in the blood." And finally, the Sartoris cavalier critique is limited not only in being overly abstract and merely stylistic but also for failing to distinguish between the historical plantation and its myth. This distinction, which would become the focus of *Absalom, Absalom!*, is however partly indicated in *Sartoris* by Faulkner's depiction of the supporting members of the plantation cast.

[20] Stark Young, *So Red the Rose* (New York, 1963), p. 197. This novel was originally published in 1934 and is therefore contemporary with both *The Unvanquished* and *Absalom, Absalom!*; see also *So Red the Rose*, pp. 67–68.

[21] *So Red the Rose*, p. 197.   [22] *Sartoris*, pp. 312–13.

Three of these, the cavalier's humble-farmer-friend, his loyal-black-servant, and his exemplary wife, have doubles in the story who are in fact alternate and antithetical versions of themselves. There is, as usual in the tradition of plantation fiction, a local farmer who defends the Sartoris hegemony and wears his own poverty with dignity, his lined face "browned and cheerful these many years with the simple and abounding earth" (p. 194). But another lower-class white man, V. K. Suratt, is less good-humored about it. In one incident Bayard and Suratt have occasion to share a jug of bootleg whiskey. As they squat behind a barn taking swallows by turn, Suratt becomes sarcastically deferential to Bayard, whom he calls "Mister Bayard," adding: " 'you'll have to excuse me. I reckon I ought to said Cap'n Sartoris, oughtn't I?' " And when Bayard objects angrily to the taunting "Mister," Suratt says wearily to another poor-white farmer,

"I knowed he was all right, when you got to know him, . . . I been knowin' him since he was knee-high to a grasshopper, but me and him jest ain't been throwed together like this. I was raised a pore boy, fellers, while Mr. Bayard's folks has lived on that 'ere big place with plenty of money in the bank and niggers to wait on 'em. But he's all right. . . . He ain't goin' to say nothin' about who give him this here whiskey." (p. 134)

The brooding tone of this passage receives some clarification from Suratt's account of his early life, but the curiously inconsistent narrative introduction to the story reveals how tentative Faulkner's consciousness of the theme still is.

Suratt's slow, plausible voice went on steadily, but without any irritant quality. It seemed to fit easily into the still scene, speaking of earthy things. "way I learnt to chop cotton," he was saying, "my oldest brother taken and put me in the row ahead of him. Started me off, and soon's I taken a lick or two, here he comes behind me. And ever' time my hoe chopped once, I could hear hisn chop twice. I never had no shoes in them days, neither," he said drily. "So I had to learn to chop fast, with that 'ere hoe of hisn cuttin' at my bare heels. But I swo' then, come what mought, I would never plant nothin' in the ground, soon's I could h'p myself. It's all right fer folks that owns the land, but folks like my folks was don't never own no land, and ever' time we made a furrow, we was scratchin' dirt fer somebody else." (p. 133)

The bitterness of the disinherited white farmer would figure prominently in later works, such as *The Mansion*. But it arises almost incidentally in *Sartoris* without introduction or development, as if Faulkner were not quite sure what to do with this bit of Bayard's environment, sensing only that it was somehow involved in his tormented story. Yet the way Suratt's brief scene springs to life reveals Faulkner's deep interest in the subject and his awareness of a deeper level in the typed character of the white farmer.

Faithful black Simon is a model Southern family servant, self-important and identifying completely with his master (warning an upstart carriage driver out of his way, Simon lectures: " 'Block off de commonality, ef you wants, but don't intervoke no equipage waitin' on Cunnel or Miss Jenny. Dey won't stan fer it' "— p. 45). As another Southerner wrote, the black man's "vices have the charm of amiable weaknesses, he is a pain and a grief to live with, a solace and a delight." [23] But Simon's son, Caspey, just returned from World War I service in a French labor battalion, is not so charming:

"I don't take nothin' fum no white folks no mo'. . . . War done changed all dat. If us cullud folks is good enough ter save France fum de Germans, den us is good enough ter have de same rights Germans is. French folks think so, anyhow, and ef America don't, dey's ways of learnin' 'um . . . War unloosed de black man's mouf. . . . Give him de right to talk. Kill Germans, den do yo' oratin', dey tole us. Well, us done it." (p. 73)

Again Faulkner seems to be writing more seriously and sensitively than he may realize, for he comments on Caspey's new ideas as if they constituted only another black's "amiable weakness." Caspey's experiences in Europe were "rather to his future detriment," Faulkner remarks lightly, and after the war he "returned to his native land a total loss, sociologically speaking, with a definite disinclination toward labor, honest or otherwise, and two honorable wounds incurred in a razor-edged crap game" (p. 73). Still, some apprehensive sense of the serious implications of Caspey's attitude must have inspired Faulkner's attitude toward a black man who is ostensibly only a fool churlishly making demands out of no deeper impulse than lazy arrogance. What Caspey is really after anyway becomes perfectly clear when he itemizes the equality he seeks, including " 'de women too, I got my white in France, and I'm gwine get it here, too.' " But in the end, even Simon's cozy

[23] William Alexander Percy, *Lanterns on the Levee, Recollections of a Planter's Son* (New York, 1950), p. 21.

humor—" 'whut us niggers want ter be free fer, anyhow? Ain't we got ez many white folks now ez we kin suppo't?' " (pp. 76, 89)—cannot quite override the mutterings of that "no 'count" Caspey:

"War showed de white folks dey can't get along widout de cullud man. Tromple him in de dus', but when de trouble bust loose, hit's 'Please, su, Mr. Cullud Man! right dis way whar de bugle blowin', Mr. Cullud Man; you is de savior of de country.' And now de cullud race gwine reap de benefits of de war, and dat soon." (p. 89)

Clearly all is not right in the master's kitchen—or, for that matter, his parlor and bedroom.

For the Southern woman who had, unlike the cavalier, fulfilled her ideal role throughout her fictional plantation life [24] seems in *Sartoris* to be faltering under the strain: she has developed an "id." Narcissa—note the name—gleams properly cool and serene in her straight white dresses, but her secret fascination with certain obscene letters suggests a weakness, if not an outright crack, in the facade. Her quasi-incestuous domination of her brother, her self-possessed calm that sometimes becomes brooding, suggest the conventional traits of the Southern belle (serenity and a moralizing influence on the men about her) grown over-ripe and perversely exaggerated. Narcissa's innocent purity has worn thin in spots through which one glimpses a darker, more knowing woman. And yet this shadowy alter ego has no overt place in the story; rather, like Suratt and Caspey, it hints at a reality behind the world of the novel, but somehow connected with the inability of Bayard to find solace in Jefferson and its good people.

[24] Taylor, p. 142.

Other corollaries of the plantation myth, such as the gentleman's vaunted rhetorical powers, have also gone awry in *Sartoris*. Rhetoric in the Sartoris household is mostly Miss Jenny's province, although old Bayard, the young Bayard's grandfather,[25] holds his ground creditably. But the oratorical skills of these two representatives of the Old South serve only for what Simon calls "quoilin'." All through the story "the concussion of Miss Jenny's raging and old Bayard's rocklike stubbornness" reverberate in the tormented house. In one way the elaborateness of these arguments is comic; but heard through the ears of the young Bayard they contribute to a finally unbearable situation: " 'let up, let up,' he howl[s], 'for God's sake, I can't hear myself chew, even' " (p. 201). Significantly when Bayard runs away to the McCallum homestead after the death of his grandfather he values especially the placid quiet that bathes these stout hunters and yeomen. At their rough board, "they ate with silent and steady decorum, with only the barest essential words, but amicably" (p. 268). That superior ability to use words which in literary tradition embodies the planter's claim to a general supremacy, has become in the Sartoris house one of the chief expressions of its unresigned inadequacy. And it is of obvious interest that a writer should represent chaos and impotence by an excessive use of words, preferring the peace of inarticulateness, all the more when that writer seems at times, like his characters, word-mad and obsessively rhetorical.

Unlike Miss Jenny's surface criticism of the "Sartoris"

[25] This Bayard Sartoris is not the Carolina Bayard mourned by Aunt Jenny but the grandfather of the Bayard who broods over his twin's death in *Sartoris*.

cavalier, Suratt, Caspey, and Narcissa challenge the essence, the substance of their respective prototypes. The poor Southerner is either a Falls or a Suratt, the black cannot be simultaneously both Simon and Caspey, and Narcissa's sexual vulnerability is irrevocably compromising. Suratt, Caspey, and Narcissa are alter-types to the traditional plantation typology and their appearance in *Sartoris* introduces into the novel the conflict between the cavalier myth and a reality (described abundantly in recent Southern histories) [26] in which the poor white farmer was bitterly discontented, the slave did yearn for freedom, and the Southern belle resented the chivalric cult that enslaved as it enshrined her. Beginning with a critique of the values of the myth and the style of life it endorsed, Faulkner was coming to question its basic validity. This tentative separation from the ruling traditions of his region was full of possibilities for Faulkner, although *Sartoris* barely begins to develop them. Neither slavery nor the plantation as a socioeconomic unit appear here except in one confused segment when we learn with surprise (because the matter has not otherwise come up) that Bayard has tried and failed to function as a planter. "For a time," Faulkner writes, "the earth had held Bayard in a hiatus that might have been called contentment."

He was up at sunrise, planting things in the ground and watching them grow and tending them; he cursed and harried niggers and mules into motion and kept them there,

[26] See especially Kenneth Stampp, *The Peculiar Institution; Slavery in the Ante-Bellum South* (New York, 1956), and, for discussions of the post-War continuation of Southern class conflicts, Albert D. Kirwan, *Revolt of the Rednecks: Mississippi Politics: 1876–1925* (Lexington, Ky., 1951), and C. Vann Woodward, *Tom Watson, Agrarian Rebel* (New York, 1963).

and put the grist mill into running shape and taught Caspey to drive the tractor, and came in at mealtimes and at night smelling of machine oil and of stables and of the earth, and went to bed with grateful muscles and with the sober rhythms of the earth in his body and so to sleep. But he still waked at times in the peaceful darkness of his room and without previous warning, tense and sweating with the old terror. (p. 181)

Why and how does the "old terror" threaten the temporary peace that Bayard has achieved? How are the two related? Clearly both situations are deeply meaningful to Faulkner, for his description of Bayard's plunge into farming, amounting almost to immersion in the earth itself, is charged with romantic emotions. The structure of the second sentence in the passage, with its accumulation of "ands," reflects the intensity not only of Bayard's activity but of the author's own feelings. But the passage merely juxtaposes the peacefulness of farming with Bayard's paralyzing terror without showing why, how, or if they interact. When Bayard's nightmares again engulf his temporary daydream, his relation to agriculture is broken off without having been defined. "It was like coming dazed out of sleep, out of the warm, sunny valleys where people lived into a region where cold peaks of savage despair stood bleakly above the lost valleys, among black and savage stars" (p. 183).

Faulkner treats the "warm, sunny valleys" and the peaks of despair as two separate realms. It is true that the way he describes them reveals an obscure sense of why they are mutually exclusive for Bayard: the valleys represent productive involvement in social life for they are "where people lived," while the peaks mean isolation from society and life, and this expresses Bayard's alienation from himself, his family, class, and land. But all this is very vague and fails to deal with the interesting question it implies: what in Bayard's heritage as a cavalier prevents his agrarian success and, in turn, what his agrarian social status has to do with the destructive propensities of his cavalier identity. These are the questions Faulkner seems to be trying to formulate by describing Bayard's agrarian failure, but because the novel generally restricts its analysis to the style rather than the substance of cavalier life, he lacks the frame of reference to do so.

The Sound and the Fury, coming next, demythologized the young aristocrat. Where Bayard Sartoris was for the most part only another version of the legendary cavalier, Quentin Compson is a more modern character trying merely to make moral sense out of the doom which has overtaken his family. If he attaches undue symbolic value to his sister's virginity, it is less for the sake of cavalier values than out of a need for a point of moral reference amid the increasing anomie of his surroundings. But, as if coming closer to the reality of the cavalier's inadequacy had triggered a general skepticism in Faulkner, *The Sound and the Fury* is at once tentatively historical and uncertain about the significance of history. Even more radically, it implicitly questions the validity of literary statements and the value of language. (Later Faulkner would explain the four separate sections of the novel as successive failures to tell a single story.) [27]

This skepticism marks an acute phase in Faulkner's

[27] *Faulkner in the University* (Class Conferences at the University of Virginia, 1957–58), ed. Frederick L. Gwynn and Joseph L. Blotner (New York, 1965), p. i.

tensely uncertain attitude toward the South and therefore toward his writing about it. But ironically, the novels of this period, *The Sound and the Fury* and *As I Lay Dying,* have been taken to represent the essential Faulkner who emerges as a prophet of the modern angst beset by doubts about the meaning of meaning and the uncertainties of linguistic communication. Thus a critic has recently written that "the basic emphasis in . . . Faulkner is not upon some ultimate ideal of truth or reality, or even upon some standard ideological dichotomy or paradox, but upon the unreality of imaginative structure of any sort and upon the radical linguistic nature—as opposed to ideological nature—of the problem of order." [28]

The dichotomy of ideology and language is a familiar one, especially in the several kinds of formalism where it functions to exclude ideological questions. Made to choose, what critic would declare himself unconcerned with the literary values of his text? But actually, if the dichotomy is ever valid, it certainly isn't for Faulkner, whose formal, linguistic problems in defining the Yoknapatawpha universe are (as I will try to show in subsequent chapters) inextricably ideological as well. In *The Sound and the Fury* with respect to the aristocratic South and, in a parallel way, in the redneck *As I Lay Dying,* Faulkner explores the limits of perception and language precisely because like Melville's Ahab he is driven to pierce false masks, the myths which he is coming more and more to realize have distorted Southern reality. In other words, Faulkner cares so much about perception in these novels because there is something he wants to see clearly but can't. His examina-

[28] Guetti, p. 11.

tions of personal visions are thus directed outward to a public landscape. Bayard Sartoris, Quentin Compson, and Addie Bundren all try to penetrate the surrounding gloom, to communicate with reality not for the sake of communication but in order to know. Indeed they might even have found some comfort in the idea that there was no truth behind the one they created themselves, but Faulkner refuses to yield them (and himself) that comparative safety. Their terrified urgency expresses instead their reluctant recognition that the resistant, mysterious world about them is also inescapably real.

It is true that these characters also try to escape that recognition by projecting worlds outside history such as the inchoate universe of the idiot Benjy and the timeless realm of his brother Quentin. Quentin does argue that time is merely a "mechanical progression" without inherent significance. He refers to objectively measured time and to the concept of causality as masks concealing reality. There is a clock time and there is a real time existing within each individual mind: "clocks slay time; only when the clock stops does time come to life." [29] He therefore breaks his watch and withdraws into his own mind where events and sensations exist statically suspended until they suddenly cease to exist at all.

Quentin is here making a Bergsonian distinction between duration and externally flowing, measurable time. Bergson defines duration as an internally experienced time measured not by clocks or other external standards, but according to one's internal consciousness. Since this personal time measures only an individual's awareness of an event or experience, it is not, as clock time is, a medium of

[29] William Faulkner, *The Sound and the Fury* (New York, 1959), p. 71.

constant flux and process, but rather a static, if extended, single moment. In Bergson's words, "duration is essentially the continuation of that which no longer exists into that which exists now." [30] Thus duration actually negates the passage of time; Quentin's argument, that the only real time is duration, transforms history into mere illusion, a period of daydreaming. And because ordering reality according to duration rather than external time is necessarily a completely individual act, it tends to make social relationships as well as historical situations merely accidental poses of no necessary relevance to an individual's inner self. But *The Sound and the Fury* also makes it clear that there is no way out of history and time but in death; Quentin breaks his watch and dies. The novel clearly warns us against adopting his views.

But it cannot itself transcend those views, and so, caught on behalf of its characters between a deadly history and personal annihilation, it becomes hopelessly paralyzed and can only repeat itself over and over. (The famous Dilsey episode, something of a Hallelujah chorus, is really no more redemptive than any other section. Perhaps Faulkner realized that no degree of endurance by a nigger mammy could reverse the disintegration of the aristocratic South. The first version of the Compson story is narrated by its last male descendant, a mental incompetent castrated for the sake of public security. The second section depicts Quentin's total recall at the last moment of a life doomed at birth, and the third is told by the eldest brother, Jason, the

[30] Henri Bergson, *Durée et simultanéité; à propos de la théorie d'Einstein* (Paris, 1931), p. 62. The original text reads: "la durée est essentiellement une continuation de ce qui n'est plus dans ce qui est."

only functional Compson and Faulkner's most despicable character anywhere in the Yoknapatawpha saga.

The "irrational brutality" of the Compsons' life has been attributed by Jean-Paul Sartre to "the author's lack of any intuitive knowledge of the future." [31] For Sartre the meaning of events lies above all in their potential development; but without disputing the general validity of this view, one must question its relevance to Faulkner, whose cavalier theme is necessarily about the past. What generates the hopelessness of *The Sound and the Fury* is, on the contrary, the author's failure to visualize the past in other than the conventional terms which we have already seen contain no answers to his questions. Quentin is driven to madness finally by the apparent arbitrariness, the mechanical entropy, with which the catastrophic present has succeeded a respectable, even a proud past. Once the Compson lands and honor were intact, men were men and life was good; now even those who have retained their wealth only parody the old values. The Kentuckians Gerald Bland and his mother shrilly portray the new-money vulgarity which has incomprehensibly risen to power. Mrs. Bland loves to tell anecdotes illustrating her son's princely temperament. "I remember the one," Quentin muses suicidally, "how Gerald throws his nigger downstairs and how the nigger pled to be allowed to matriculate in the divinity school to be near marster marse Gerald and how he ran all the way to the station beside the carriage with tears in his eyes when marse Gerald rid away. . . ." [32] The Blands are

[31] Jean-Paul Sartre, "Time in Faulkner: *The Sound and the Fury*," rpt. in *William Faulkner; Three Decades of Criticism*, p. 231.

[32] *The Sound and the Fury*, p. 85.

repugnant, of course, but what makes them so? Quentin's objection to the little vignette of marse Gerald and the nigger seems to be mainly a matter of taste. Unwilling or unable to ask whether they have debased his heritage or only exposed it, he thus sticks at the execrable manners by which the Blands destroy the civilized facade he has leaned on. At this point there is not much difference between Quentin's attachment to the conventions of cavalier culture and Benjy's blind insistence on any pattern that has become familiar. As the chilling close of the novel warns, such arbitrary orders threaten imminently to dissolve into chaos. Benjy has been accustomed on his rides into town to follow a particular route counterclockwise around the square. This time his driver goes around it clockwise. Horrified by this violation of his sense of order and propriety, Benjy howls piercingly until the course of the carriage is reversed and "cornice and facade flowed smoothly once more from left to right; post and tree, window and doorway, and signboard, each in its ordered place." [33] The novel's last words, "each in its ordered place," imply radical disbelief in the meaningfulness of all orders, including necessarily the ordering vision of fiction. At this nadir of Faulkner's struggle with his own ambivalence toward the South, he seems almost ready to identify with Quentin Compson who, when he determined that life was meaningless, simply stopped.

[33] *The Sound and the Fury,* p. 224.

2

Death of the Prodigal

The two remaining cavalier novels, *Absalom, Absalom!* and *The Unvanquished,* constitute completely opposite resolutions to *The Sound and the Fury* crisis, and yet they were written almost concurrently.[1] Faulkner's progress to this point of exacerbated, polarized indecision can be traced in the development of the recalling plot which achieves its final elaboration in *Absalom, Absalom!* Here Quentin Compson evokes a complete vision of the past by working his way through myths back into their historical origins. But at the same time, dealing with the Civil War in *The Unvanquished,* Faulkner seemed to accept the conventional mythology so completely that he took it to be historical fact, a confusion which even *Sartoris* had avoided by clearly

[1] *Absalom, Absalom!* was published in 1936. Although *The Unvanquished* appeared in novel form in 1938, all but the last chapter had been published as stories in *The Saturday Evening Post* and *Scribner's Magazine* between 1934 and 1936.

labeling its subject matter as myth. The narrator of *The Un-vanquished* is an old man living in an undetermined and peaceful present pleasantly illuminated by memories of a gallant past. The climax of the novel occurs when Bayard becomes a man and shoulders the responsibilities of his class by setting a moral example in a dangerous situation which he survives triumphantly. It is thus effectively an anti-recalling plot which negates the form's original motive which is to discover the source of the hero's doom. For in *The Unvanquished* the recalled past is instead redemptive.

The novel is composed of seven chronological episodes in the life of Bayard Sartoris who is the grandfather in *Sartoris*. They begin just after the fall of Vicksburg and continue through the period of Reconstruction to about 1876. We see the Sartorises stand up stoutly to these trials, keeping their backs straight and their ammunition dry. "It was hard to make the Civil War seem cosy," Edmund Wilson has observed, "but Thomas Nelson Page did his best." [2] Faulkner's best in that vein does not quite match Page's but *The Unvanquished* does a creditable job. The plantation world glows warmly out of the past, certainly happier and more harmonious than most. If slavery was on the whole iniquitous, the Sartoris slaves were better off than the freed blacks of the post-War chaos. (Bayard once watches hundreds of freed slaves march past, seeking the River Jordan; when some among them fall on the road, others walk right over them, finally to drown like lemmings when they come to a stream, and are quite unable to stop or shift directions.) Perhaps the most telling aspect of *The Unvanquished* is its resurrection of John Sartoris, the ghost

[2] Edmund Wilson, *Patriotic Gore, Studies in the Literature of the American Civil War* (New York, 1962), pp. 613–14.

who briefly dominated the opening pages of *Sartoris* and seemed there to forecast just another nostalgic celebration of the cavalier myth. In *Sartoris*, however, John Sartoris was immediately thrust into the background by the more complex figure of his great-grandson through whom the story became correspondingly more interesting. Here John Sartoris towers unrivaled, for Faulkner, who said once that the deeply subversive *Absalom, Absalom!* was the hardest of his books to write, seems to have found periodic respite in the affirmative stories of *The Unvanquished.*

The novel's concluding episode illustrates the apologies that inform all seven. The setting is this: John Sartoris has returned from the Civil War to find Yoknapatawpha County overrun by carpetbaggers. He organizes his friends into a band of Nightriders who restore order. They terrorize "the niggers," kill two Washington envoys and, on the occasion of the county's first election, steal the ballot boxes. They do all this despite their own distaste for dirty dealing because it is necessary for the good of the community. Faulkner establishes the moral stature of John Sartoris by having him then renounce violence once the power of the landowners has been restored. "Now," he announces, "I shall do a little moral housecleaning. I am tired of killing men, no matter what the necessity or the end." [3] In his "naïveté," Sutpen might have wondered about the lately repentant Colonel, but Faulkner's straight rendition of the conversion (and there is no way, I think, that one can read it ironically) dramatizes the limitation on his vision which the John Sartoris logos imposed. Sartoris has a mortal enemy, however, a man named Ben Redmond with whom he had developed Mississippi's new railroad before, as the

[3] William Faulkner, *The Unvanquished* (New York, 1961), p. 175.

better man, he won it all.[4] The resentful Redmond kills Sartoris, and the last chapter describes Bayard's response to the murder of his father. Bayard turns to God and to nonviolence, for "if there was anything at all in the Book anything of hope and peace for His blind and bewildered spawn which He had chosen above all to offer immortality, *Thou shalt not kill* must be it." [5] He goes, therefore, unarmed to the duel he has arranged with Redmond. As it almost always will, if not in such as *Absalom, Absalom!*, good triumphs and Redmond is converted. He shoots over the youth's head and then throws away his gun forever.

One might expect from the uncritical way in which Faulkner depicts the cavalier legend in *The Unvanquished* that its language would be equally stylized and prone to exaggeration. But this is not at all the case. On the contrary, Bayard is a scrupulously realistic narrator carefully explaining that "Father was not big. It was just the things he did, . . . that made him seem bigger to us" (p. 17). The effect is obvious: a Napoleonic Sartoris is the bigger man for Bayard's disclaimer, having gained spiritual stature at the cost of mere physical inches. In fact and in a manner which might at first seem paradoxical, with each of these realistic qualifications Bayard only propels his father's legendary character a little farther from reality. For example, he remembers as a boy helping his father put up a stock-pen with what had then seemed to him miraculous speed. Grown-up, he realizes that it "only" took hard and efficient

[4] The most valuable gloss on this episode is to be found in C. Vann Woodward's *Origins of the New South, 1877–1913*. He describes the triumvirate of L. Q. C. Lamar, Edward C. Walthall, and James Z. George, who established the first Redeemer administration in Mississippi as primarily industrial investors with a special concentration in railroads.

[5] *The Unvanquished*, p. 165.

labor. But if anything is more impressive than magic, it is being able without a wand to make things seem magical. Bayard has neither qualified nor modified the John Sartoris myth; all he has done is to translate the fairy tale into adult terms. The uncharacteristically clear, moderate tone in which Faulkner wrote *The Unvanquished* has just this function vis-à-vis the myth it extols. Failing (or refusing) in this work to distinguish between myth and history, he does away rhetorically with the distinction itself and achieves a general credibility through a language which seems sufficiently reasonable (or perhaps only bland enough) to be factual.

The language of *Absalom, Absalom!*, on the other hand, seems the very stuff of myth, its characters grotesque and its situations incredible. The first description of the hero, Thomas Sutpen, is not only mythical but a very compendium of myths. He was a "man horse demon," a being "not articulated in this world." "He was a walking shadow. He was the light-blinded bat-like image of his own torment cast by the fierce demoniac lantern up from beneath the earth's crust . . ." [6] Of course this passage occurs near the beginning of the book when Sutpen is still only a legend. But even when his "real" self emerges, the writing remains as fantastical as ever—and therein lies an important but frequently misinterpreted aspect of Faulkner's style. Describing the rigors of reading Faulkner, Joseph Warren Beach expresses this general view:

Half the time we are swimming under water, holding our breath and straining our eyes to read off the meaning of submarine phenomena, unable to tell fact from figure, to

[6] William Faulkner, *Absalom, Absalom!* (New York, 1951), p. 171.

fix the reference of pronouns, or distinguish between guess and certainty. From time to time we come to the surface, gasping, to breathe the air of concrete fact and recorded truth, only to go floundering again the next moment through crashing waves of doubt and speculation.[7]

But, to borrow Beach's image, I suspect that it is actually when we are deepest under water—and we never dive deeper than in *Absalom, Absalom!*—that we are most likely to discover "concrete fact" or more precisely an account of history which Faulkner intends us to accept as reliable. Even when in *The Sound and the Fury* he questioned the validity of individual perception of the external world, he was motivated by the assumption that it mattered a great deal to see that world clearly. In *Absalom, Absalom!* he is after the same thing, a reliable portrait of reality: out of the memories of unreliable witnesses Quentin derives a quite plausible account of the life of Thomas Sutpen, an account which Faulkner then validates. The prevalent reading of *Absalom, Absalom!* has been that "the Sutpen tragedy as communicated in the novel has no 'objective' existence"; it "rests upon unreality." [8] But it does, in fact, achieve a reliable and tangible reality, and even a credibility that triumphs (making Faulkner's point the more vivid) over the incredible events of Sutpen's story. In *The Unvanquished*, as we saw, the rhetoric of moderation disguises Bayard's immoderate valuation of his father; in *Absalom, Absalom!* we are urged to recognize the impossible extravagance with which Sutpen has been described because Faulkner

[7] Joseph Warren Beach, *American Fiction: 1920–1940, 1941,* cited in Introduction of *William Faulkner: Three Decades of Criticism,* p. 23.

[8] Ilse Dusoir Lind, "The Design and Meaning of *Absalom, Absalom!*" rpt. in *William Faulkner; Three Decades of Criticism,* pp. 281–82.

intends to make this extravagance the measure of an extraordinary reality. In short, where in the first instance a plain prose style renders fantasy credible, in the second, extravagant writing evokes a world which is incredible but, in Faulkner's view, historically all too accurate. We move in *Absalom, Absalom!* from myth to history and discover that history is more fantastic than any myth—predictably so perhaps since myth is a more ordered, selective interpretation of events which in this case attacked the very sanity of those who experienced them.

At the end of the process by which Quentin Compson finally arrives at the history of the Sutpens, his companion in the quest asks what is for him a logical final question: "Why do you hate the South?" Why else, he implies, would Quentin probe the depths of its iniquities so ruthlessly? Quentin's answer closes the book on an anti-rational note that finally transcends all the reasons and ordered visions contained in the myths he has debunked, to affirm for a timeless moment (in a dimension below myth and even history, being the pure experience prior to both) an uninterpreted, uninterpretable fact: "I dont hate it! I dont hate it!" From myth to history to raw experience, the content of the novel moves away from abstraction toward unique, precise, concrete fact. In the face of all the constructs and hypotheses that have emerged in the course of the story, Quentin's assertion that he does not hate the South is merely or at last true, self-sufficient and opaque, neither echoing nor really resonant.

Thus the linguistic elaborateness of Faulkner's style which has been taken to reflect abstract, purely literary concerns, is rather tooled to the demands of a complex and divided social vision. Because he is always trying to find a way to say something, or even to decide what he wants to say—rather than exploring language reflexively—his highest linguistic flights delve deepest into Southern life. I am not suggesting of course that Faulkner wrote in a complicated style because he had complicated things to say, but only that his convoluted sentences did lead outward, in constant quest for what he considered the real world. Conversely, in its author's characteristic idiom, the simplicity of *The Unvanquished* expresses a lack of engagement with the material and the writing. There are passages when Faulkner seems not to be paying attention. Near the end of the novel, for instance, there is an episode which should have been highly dramatic but is really only a little puzzling. The legendary Colonel Sartoris has married a much younger woman, Drusilla, who makes advances to the Colonel's son Bayard, the hero of *The Unvanquished*. The theme of incest appears prominently in *Absalom, Absalom!* where it is functional on many levels. Here, however, Faulkner appears uncertain as to why he has even raised the issue; their first embrace causes Bayard to reflect cleverly on "the woman of thirty," "the symbol of the ancient and eternal Snake and of the men who have written of her, and I realized then the immitigable chasm between all life and all print—that those who can, do, those who cannot and suffer because they can't, write about it." [9]

This has nothing to do with anything—either in or out of the novel. One's suspicion at this point that the author has his mind elsewhere is strengthened when Bayard speculates that unlike men, women do not have common responses to events but remain "incorrigibly individual." But Drusilla precisely is a type and so functions in the story to

[9] *The Unvanquished,* p. 173.

represent the familiar category of young, erstwhile belles who toughened their hands and hearts serving the Confederacy. This is all rather symptomatic than intrinsically important; what it represents is Faulkner not writing: keeping his own account of things superficial so as not to engage either the deeper meanings latent in his material. *Absalom, Absalom!*, in contrast, represents the stylistic, formal fruition of the author's deep, if anachronistic, concern for the substance, the "message" in his writing.

Of all his works, this is the one which most explicitly and directly sets out to discover something, to find out what really happened. It is in fact plotted something like a detective story leading us toward revelations that are withheld until the last pages. It is in this work that Faulkner achieves the final unfolding of the recalling plot. Stylistically, *Absalom, Absalom!* spirals into confusing, sometimes self-parodying complexities. But this is also Faulkner's best work, the high point of his career which finally realized that potential we have traced unfolding in preceding stories but, paradoxically, was to be itself a sort of dead end. The most important of the writings following *Absalom, Absalom!* are the three Snopes novels and these show a marked shift in perspective toward a more conventional sociology and a more traditional style. The trilogy will be the subject of the last chapters, although it may be useful to mention here that following the apotheosis which *Absalom, Absalom!* constitutes of his attempts to recapture the past, Faulkner took the logical next step and moved his fictional theater to the present. But then, rather than continuing his survey of Southern experience along the critical lines developed through the earlier writings, the later works tended to negate all the conclusions he had already reached, by depicting the present in such a way as necessarily to imply a past not like that of *Absalom, Absalom!* but of the apologetic *The Unvanquished.*

Absalom, Absalom!, then, is an attempt to uncover the truth behind certain legends. Quentin Compson takes on this task against his will in a way already familiar from *Soldiers' Pay, Sartoris,* and *The Sound and the Fury.* Rosa Coldfield, the dead Sutpen's aging sister-in-law, asks Quentin to accompany her on a mysterious journey to the decaying family mansion. He recalls stories he heard as a boy about the demoniac Thomas Sutpen, once a rich and powerful planter, who suffered a catastrophic fall shortly after the Civil War, for reasons no one seems to fully understand. Miss Coldfield, Quentin finds, burns with avenging hatred for Sutpen, and her mission has something to do with wreaking that hate upon him. Gradually Quentin recognizes his own history in the story of the Sutpens, a dark heritage he'll never escape. From Miss Coldfield and from his world-weary alcoholic father he tries to learn exactly who Sutpen was and what really happened to him, but neither source is at all reliable. Each one constructs a story according to her or his predilections; Rosa Coldfield's seems patterned on the Old Testament [10] while Mr. Compson's version is redolent with exotic characters and complex machinations. Limited to the information he can glean from his dubious informants and burdened too by his own deepening emotional stake in the story, Quentin painfully re-

---

[10] Rosa Coldfield's God is peculiarly vengeful. Thus she stresses that Sutpen's first meeting with her sister (whom he would later marry) took place in a church "as though there were a fatality and curse on our family and God Himself were seeing to it that it was performed and discharged to the last drop and dreg" (*Absalom, Absalom!*, p. 21).

constructs an account we come to accept as what must have happened.

It has been generally argued, as Ilse Lind put it succinctly, that the Sutpen tragedy as communicated in the novel has no objective existence. "It is the collective product of the workings of the minds of three major narrators abetted by the collaboration of a fourth." [11] The three major narrators Lind refers to are, of course, Rosa Coldfield, Mr. Compson senior, and Quentin. The fourth is a roommate of Quentin's at Harvard, a Canadian named Shreve McCannon to whom Quentin is speaking throughout the last two-thirds of the novel. But the three Southern narrators are not of equal stature. Actually Quentin is very much in the foreground, with the other two more and more only providing the material out of which he composes the final story. We are made to care about Quentin much more than about the others and also to pay greater heed to his analysis of the Sutpen legend. For critics committed to rigorous definitions of "persona" and "narrative point of view," all the *Absalom, Absalom!* narrators may fall into one category since none of them is omniscient. But reading is not so legalistic an enterprise as that, and in reading *Absalom, Absalom!* one cannot avoid seeing a hierarchy among the narrations. Perhaps we ought not to lend most credence to Quentin but we do, which can only be, after all, because of something Faulkner does. And what Faulkner does is really the point, not what a lawyer would make of it.

Liberal criticism tends to dwell perhaps too much on the individual points of view of characters, assuming that all fictional worlds are blessed with Anglo-Saxon pluralism.

[11] Lind, pp. 281–82.

The view that *Absalom, Absalom!* simply offers many ways of looking at the Sutpens without finally opting for any one seems to reflect this assumption, which also has informed the view that *The Sound and the Fury* (and *As I Lay Dying*, for that matter) expresses a very literary (literarist?) fascination with the infinite multiplicity of perceptions possible. But as I suggested earlier, it is not fascination but pain which animates *The Sound and the Fury*, and despair of ever really knowing truly how things are because they appear so different to different people. Faulkner's attitude may thus recall Melville's in *The Confidence Man*, that nightmare of pluralistic, individualistic America. *Absalom, Absalom!* similarly holds no brief for pluralistic interpretations, but desperately seeks the truth. Indeed it violates the spirit and the emotional tone of Faulkner's writing either in *The Sound and the Fury* or in *Absalom, Absalom!* to conclude from the difficulties he encountered in achieving a narrative synthesis that he was not really seeking one.

The view that any perception is hopelessly biased and the past forever out of reach, that we can never know anything about others because the meaning of their behavior lies outside the shared assumptions that language requires, is assigned, in the novel, to Mr. Compson, who neurotically avoids all certainties, all definite statements and all decisive acts. Trying half-heartedly to piece together the Sutpen story, the elder Compson shrugs that "it just does not explain." "Or perhaps," he goes on, "that's it: they don't explain and we are not supposed to know." All the separate details are like "a chemical formula":

"you bring them together in the proportions called for, but nothing happens; you re-read, tedious and intent, poring, making sure that you have forgotten nothing, made no mis-calculation; you bring them together again and again nothing happens: just the words, the symbols, the shapes themselves, shadowy inscrutable and serene, against that turgid background of a horrible and bloody mischancing of human affairs." [12]

But Quentin, a better man than his father, does make something happen, bringing the story to life so successfully that when in the end he meets one of its participants in the flesh, the living man can fuse imperceptibly with his recreation.

In other words, Quentin differs significantly with his father's sense of history when the latter calls the Sutpen tragedy a "mischancing of human affairs," meaning that chance is the dominant factor in the lives of both individuals and communities. Nor does Quentin share Rosa Coldfield's view that it was all a matter of evil destiny. For Mr. Compson the world is ultimately inexplicable, while Miss Rosa has already read all the answers in the book of God. When in the beginning of the story it is their two versions of the Sutpen mystery which dominate (Quentin having not yet taken over), we hear repeatedly that Sutpen either "came out of nowhere," that he appeared with "no discernible past" "apparently out of nothing," or "apparently complete," or that he "abrupted" from Hell, defying all explanations or requiring none. It is interesting to note that as a child Thomas Sutpen is also unaware of having any social origin: "he knew neither where he had come from nor where he was nor why. He was just there . . ." (pp. 9, 32, 11, 93, 227). But Sutpen learns better as does Quentin—

[12] *Absalom, Absalom!*, p. 101.

and the novel goes on to postulate a coherent and comprehensible history.

A little more than a third of the way through, the narration comes definitively under Quentin's control. The locale shifts to Harvard and the room he shares with Shreve. That far from home, and with the further distancing effect of trying to explain things to his Canadian friend who shares neither his idiom nor his attitudes, Quentin begins to function as a surrogate novelist. The relationship to Shreve is an aspect of this change in Quentin's role from an unwilling listener to the book's focal creative consciousness. It may be significant that Shreve would go directly from Harvard into the Canadian Expeditionary Forces for service in wartime France and that Faulkner himself trained with the Royal Canadian Flying Corps and sometimes vaguely claimed to have served with it in France during the same period. Certainly the young Canadian blends into Quentin's narrative persona and expands it, even at one point taking over while Quentin painfully and at long intervals can mutter only "yes." Shreve's conduct of the process of reconstruction is then much less respectful than Quentin's. For instance, Shreve refers to Rosa Coldfield as "this old gal, this Aunt Rosa" while Quentin insists, "Miss Rosa" (p. 176); clearly a greater detachment from Southern compunctions is one of the things that Faulkner must add to Quentin's stance to render it capable of sustaining the role of author. Something of this is indeed indicated by Quentin's reflection, while listening to Shreve, that "if I had been there I could not have seen it this plain" (p. 190).

Thus Faulkner makes Quentin and Shreve take over so that their analysis becomes the substance of the book. He then does something which I think conclusively indicates his intention to accept their hypothesis as real: he concludes their version of the story with the incredible reappearance of one of its characters, now old and infirm but incontestably real. How this works and its significance will be more easily explained in the context of the actual Sutpen story which Quentin reconstructs.

Thomas Sutpen came from a family of "rednecks" (poor white farmers usually of Scotch-Irish ancestry) who lived in the hilly and barren northern part of Virginia (Appalachia) at the beginning of the nineteenth century. Living in isolation and ignorance, Sutpen knew of no other way of life than his own deprived but egalitarian one, until his family began a long trek South into plantation country. Then he discovered classes and his own class identity at the bottom of a social hierarchy which placed even "niggers" above him. In one incident which haunted him all his life, the fourteen-year-old Sutpen was turned away from the front door of a plantation house by a uniformed black butler who sent him around to the back. Stunned by what was at first an incomprehensible humiliation, Sutpen quickly came to understand the perversity of social ethics by which only those who did nothing useful were considered human while he and his family lived and indeed were become like brutish cattle inhabiting rotten log cabins where the children "seemed to take sick after supper and die before the next meal."

Quentin's re-creation of what Sutpen must have thought out following his epiphany before the slave mansion, although it refers to an antebellum situation, recalls the thirties literature on poor Southern whites, books like

James Agee's *Let Us Now Praise Famous Men* or the reports of the Works Progress Administration.[13] Like them it emphasizes the devaluation of labor wrought by the Southern land oligopoly. Watching his sister scrubbing clothes, Sutpen is revolted to see her like "a cow, the very labor she was doing brutish and stupidly out of all proportion to its reward: the very primary essence of labor, toil, reduced to its crude absolute which only a beast could or would endure" (p. 236). Such an attitude is not at all anachronistic; this stress on the question of the value of labor is one of the aspects of the novel which exemplifies its highly successful historicity. Long before the Civil War there were debates in the South about the social and ethical implications of a leisure class and, as I have mentioned earlier, many who were otherwise supporters of the landed aristocracy worried that excessive power over other human beings and over-abundant leisure might undermine the character of the Southern gentleman. For Northerners writing even as early as Crèvecœur, it was a frequent theme to decry the moral iniquities of cities like Charles-Town [14] where planters were said to run riot in bordellos and gambling halls. Crèvecœur is highly representative in considering the root of all this evil to be the planters' failure to partake of the sanctity of labor. This is something of an American commandment, articulated of course most notably by another Southerner, Thomas Jefferson. Nor was his idea at all alien to the South, for the majority of whites in

---

[13] See *Mississippi, A Guide to the Magnolia State,* compiled and written by the Federal Writers' Project of the Works Progress Administration (New York, 1938).

[14] See, for example, Crèvecœur, Letter ix, "Description of Charles-Town; Thoughts on Slavery; On Physical Evil; A Melancholy Scene."

the region enjoyed very little leisure and looked askance at their social betters. At the time of young Sutpen's humiliation—around 1832—debates still raged in Virginia about the continuance of slavery. It was not so much the ethic of human slavery that was being debated as the choice "between two social patterns: the plantation system with its masters and slaves, and the Jeffersonian idea, of a society of small landowners tilling their own soil." [15] Virginia, speaking here for the region, did not finally vote down abolition until 1832; the following year Thomas Sutpen established his plantation in Yoknapatawpha County. And as Faulkner explained it later, Sutpen "wanted to take revenge for all the redneck people against the aristocrat who told him to go around to the back door." [16]

Faulkner's depiction of Sutpen's encounter with the upper class is strongly sympathetic. Even later when he was less critical of aristocrats, he would express similar sympathies for the redneck Mink Snopes in his battles with a gentleman farmer. Suffused as it was with the romance of the soil, the Jeffersonian ideal clearly appealed to Faulkner, who spoke glowingly, if with some exaggeration, of his own status as a farmer.[17] But there was also a more specifically political content to the author's remarkable understanding of the redneck case. In the more common depiction of Faulkner as a Southern gentleman, it has not been sufficiently noted that he had strong ties to the hostile neo-Populist party. His uncle, whom his friend and confidant

[15] Smith, p. 152.   [16] *Faulkner in the University,* pp. 97–98.

[17] In *Faulkner at Nagano* (Tokyo, 1956), Robert A. Jelliffe describes Faulkner as speaking at some length of the farm he shared with his brother John (who managed it) and stressing his identity as a farmer: " 'I'm a country man, my life is farmland and the raising of grain and feed. . . . My life is as a farmer' " (p. 142).

Phil Stone considered an absolutely crucial influence on him, was an aide of the neo-Populist V. K. Vardaman; Faulkner's grandfather was also a Vardaman supporter.[18] Vardaman was elected by a redneck constituency on the basis of much Jeffersonian rhetoric but also some substance. Faulkner's depiction of Sutpen and of his lower-class origins must have drawn heavily on his memories of his uncle's political activities; in choosing a redneck as the focal historical figure of *Absalom, Absalom!,* which is his most complete account of the period before the Civil War, Faulkner departed from the cavalier myth to pose as the central question of Southern history, not the Civil War, but an internal conflict between agrarians, something no cavalier would have considered more than a passing and predetermined skirmish. But for Faulkner the question—plantation or Jeffersonian homestead?—was a burning issue, by whose light all of Southern history would be newly reconstructed. The real threat to Sutpen's happiness and morality, whether as a dirt-farmer or a planter (being no Yankee he would have been perfectly willing to accept a dignified economic inferiority) lies in the plantation system itself. To survive as a man he has to become a gentleman; but to become a gentleman, he must sacrifice his ethical manhood. His rise and fall, spanning the years of established plantation hegemony, thus sketches a radically critical picture of the antebellum South.

Both in terms of the material he wanted to treat and

[18] William Van O'Connor, in *The Tangled Fire of William Faulkner* (Minneapolis, 1954), quotes Phil Stone explaining that Faulkner "was born before the movement got under way and passed his life until manhood in the very middle of it, his grandfather and his only uncle being leaders in the following of Vardaman" (p. 10).

with regard to his own emotional and intellectual attitudes to this material, Faulkner could not have created a better hero than Thomas Sutpen. By striving to become the very type of the planter in order to avenge his affronted redneck dignity, Sutpen represents both Southern agrarian ideologies converging to a certain doom, whose human cost, thus concentrated in one person, can be the most vividly depicted. On one level Sutpen as lord and peasant both can embody the entire white South corrupted and ultimately destroyed by the plantation system. In the childhood episodes, Sutpen enables Faulkner to give the redneck case as I have outlined it earlier. But Thomas Sutpen as planter can also express an opposite attitude of sympathy for the aristocracy like that evident in *Sartoris*. Whereas there, however, Faulkner's sympathy blocked his exploration of the concrete realities of plantation life, here it results rather in a more complex perception of the plight of the gentleman. Indeed, with Sutpen as a focus, the more torn Faulkner feels between conflicting loyalties to planters and rednecks, and the more he empathizes with the former while voicing the complaints of the latter, the more complex and rich become the characterizations and situations of *Absalom, Absalom!* The poignancy of Sutpen's humiliated boyhood may be inspired by one set of ideas and his grandeur as a doomed but powerful planter by another— but it works. Sutpen, in short, freed Faulkner from the limitations of his ambiguity toward the past precisely by justifying an ambiguous attitude toward himself. Ambiguity here engendered a position of critical independence which was nevertheless energized by the author's sympathy.

In stressing the agrarian issue I have ignored what may appear a more prominent cause of Sutpen's downfall, his

racial attitudes. It is true that once he has made his decision to enter the plantation aristocracy, Sutpen's troubles
are mostly racial. Before coming to Yoknapatawpha, Sutpen had built up a plantation in the West Indies. Faulkner
pointedly describes him landing in Haiti ("a soil manured
with black blood") just before the slave rebellions of
1791–93 which haunted American slavers forever after. As a
reward for helping a wealthy planter put down the insur-
rection among his slaves, Sutpen earns the planter's daughter and a sizable plantation of his own. But just before the
birth of his first son he discovers that his wife has had a
black ancestor. Since she thus would bar his achievement
of a real aristocratic status, he abandons her, his son, and
his land to begin again in Mississippi. "Sutpen's Hundred,"
as he calls the plantation he builds up there, with its mansion full of imported furniture and its irreproachable
mistress (the sister of Rosa Coldfield), seems at first to ful-
fill his design. His two children, Henry and Judith, will
surely launch a Sutpen dynasty. Objectively, he has now arrived at the stage that the Southern aristocracy as a class
achieved in the early 1830's.

At this point, however, the tainted first son reappears,
perhaps unwittingly (although we are never quite sure of
this) as Henry's college friend, Charles Bon. Becoming Judith's suitor, he raises horrifying specters of incest and miscegenation. In an attempt to ward off disaster, Sutpen, who
cannot act directly without acknowledging a black man as
his son, reveals Bon's race to Henry, intending only that
the white brother drive off the black. But Henry kills Bon
and then himself disappears, leaving Sutpen without an
heir and the plantation without a future. Actually Sutpen
had first told Henry that Charles was his brother, hoping

that Henry would forbid incest. But Bon's sway over the younger man is so great that he seems about to tolerate the marriage when Sutpen in despair reveals the rest. Prepared to countenance incest, so deep is his love for his brother, Henry kills him at once to prevent miscegenation. Outside, in a kind of historical pathetic fallacy, the Civil War is raging and Sutpen and his world come crashing down together.

As a planter, Sutpen's doom is thus sealed by the racism that the slave system necessitates. But his story and his importance to *Absalom, Absalom!* begin before he becomes a planter and continue after the destruction of "Sutpen's Hundred" when he tries once more to achieve the only real status available in his society by rebuilding his estate. Needing a male heir to ensure his aristocratic descent, he turns, ironically, to the granddaughter of Wash Jones, one of his "redneck" employees. But she bears him a daughter and he abandons her. This time it is all over: Wash, who had until then, regarded Sutpen as the apotheosis of lower-class dreams, now kills him in a fury of humiliated disillusionment that recalls Sutpen's own boyhood trauma. *"Better if his kind and mine too had never drawn breath of life on this earth,"* Wash Jones sobs as he strikes Sutpen. Better that than that another of his miserable, humiliated kind should *"see his whole life shredded from him and shrivel away like a dried shuck thrown onto the fire"* (pp. 290–91).

The wheel, driven round by the imbalances in its own construction, has come full circle with the vengeance of a redneck on a gentleman who trampled his dignity. Sutpen is killed by a man who might have been himself. Thus it is really the agrarian class conflict which initiates, motivates, and concludes Sutpen's career, with problems of race set, as it were, parenthetically within its broader context. I think this represents Faulkner's attitude generally, his view being essentially that race and even slavery were issues within the white class conflict and perhaps more destructive because of that context than they would have been otherwise. In other words, it was not the plight of black slaves that worried him most but their impact on the structure of white society. And this already primary concern with problems of class later dominated Faulkner's thinking even more. There are virtually no black characters in the Snopes stories, which focus instead on shifting class relations among whites as the crucial issue for the New South.

As is evident even in this brief summary of Sutpen's story, it is characterized by a kind of irony which operates to turn everything he does against him. This irony is activated by Sutpen's ignorance of the forces with which he deals or his incomplete understanding of them. Indeed this is the hallmark of his career, beginning with his surprise at encountering upper-class snobbery and ending in a fatal lack of awareness that even hirelings have feelings. Faulkner stresses Sutpen's ignorance, describing him, for instance, in Haiti "not knowing that what he rode upon was a volcano," for he "believed that earth was kind and gentle" (p. 251). Mr. Compson remembers his own father, who knew Sutpen, saying that his chief trait was an enduring "naiveté, innocence." This quality in his protagonist is useful in enabling Faulkner to reveal the darker realities of the plantation system as they manifest themselves to thwart Sutpen's expectations. Like the lush fertility of Haiti, sprung "with an incredible paradox" out of "torn limbs and outraged hearts," the social success he wants will necessi-

tate his destroying the lives of others. Since he doesn't realize this at the start, or at least not fully, its coming about
dramatizes the more vividly its structural, organic inevita-
bility.[19]

Thematically, the education of Thomas Sutpen parallels
that of Quentin, who, however, suspects all along that the
truth is deadly. Thus, in Sutpen's career we see the substance, the goal of the recalling plot, the fatal situation still
in the making, the innocence not yet lost, while simultaneously the novel shows us Quentin after the fact, re-creat-
ing it. In the end the two processes will come together
when Quentin uncovers the last details of Sutpen's tragedy
and himself plays a role in it. But the fusion of these two
levels of the novel is mutually annihilative for their protagonists and closes the story. Henry dies immediately afterwards in the fiery destruction of "Sutpen's Hundred"
and Quentin goes back to Harvard, there to commit suicide
only a few months later.

One would not ordinarily append the conclusion of
one novel to the plot of another and it is true that Quentin
does not kill himself in *Absalom, Absalom!* But Faulkner
clearly intends us to recall the earlier suicide in the context
of this later story when he writes in its "Genealogy" that
Quentin Compson "attended Harvard 1909–1910. Died
Cambridge, Mass., 1910," thus at the end of the semester
during which he and Shreve reconstructed the Sutpen
legend. The coincidence of names would be meaningful
even if Faulkner did not so carefully date events in *Absalom, Absalom!* so that they dovetail with *The Sound and*

[19] Cleanth Brooks in *The Yoknapatawpha Country* argues on the contrary that since Sutpen is atypical, he does not directly reflect on the
Southern plantation system *per se*.

the Fury. But especially since he does, it would seem perverse (or perhaps merely pedantic) not to connect the two Quentins so that the experience of recreating the Sutpen tragedy is seen to have contributed significantly to his suicide. Quentin's involvement in the fate of the Sutpens is significantly deepened through his empathy with Henry, whom he resembles in important respects. Henry, like Quentin, had been the family heir, the one who had to confront the crisis his forebears had bequeathed him and who, by implementing their values, damns himself and dooms his family. Quentin need not have made the same decision of course, but he is forced to recognize the relevance of Henry's tragic dilemma to his own uncertain feelings about Southern traditions.

Quentin's identification with Henry accomplishes the purpose of the *Sartoris* doubling of the central figure in the recalling plot: Quentin has a deep personal stake in the events he is reconstructing but he also stands sufficiently apart to view them as history. And now with one last alteration the structure of the recalling plot is made fully responsive to Faulkner's intent to treat history as if it still matters and indeed survives yet. He allows Quentin to meet a still living Henry who, as if resurrected, appears to affirm the inescapable reality of the past. After that, there can be for Quentin "Nevermore of peace. Nevermore Nevermore Nevermore." The man he finds in the house to which Rosa Coldfield leads him (the suspicion that he was there, a surviving Sutpen from whom she could exact revenge, turns out to have been the reason she had requisitioned Quentin) is only barely alive; Quentin recalls "the wasted hands crossed on the breast as if he were already a corpse." But the blurring of life and death here represents their fusion, as the deadly past engulfs the present. Or, in Quentin's words, "waking or sleeping it was the same and would be the same forever as long as he lived" (p. 373). The brief liturgical exchange between the two men, in its cyclically repetitive form, embodies the sense of achieved doom, the now fully realized goal of the recalling plot:

> And you are . . . ?
> Henry Sutpen.
> And you have been here . . . ?
> Four years.
> And you came home . . . ?
> To die. Yes.
> To die?
> Yes. To die.
> And you have been here . . . ?
> Four years.
> And you are . . . ?
> Henry Sutpen. (p. 373)

What I want especially to stress here is the validating effect of this meeting. Not that Henry's reappearance vouches for the details of Quentin's hypothetical recreation, but that is not necessary anyway to give the Sutpen tragedy an "objective" existence. Henry's wasted but indubitably real body provides instead an external fact which establishes the Sutpen legend in the real world. The fusion of life and death expressed in Quentin's anguished recognition that "waking or sleeping it was the same" is also the fusion of objective and subjective realities into one wholly real experience. Earlier Faulkner described the sense of unreality within which Quentin and Shreve wove their own version "out of the rag-tag and bob-ends of old tales and talking" (p. 303). The introduction of a living Henry Sutpen could only express the author's intention to lend substance to their thesis. Before this they lack evidence that the story they have concocted has any objective validity or is anything but a myth about "people who perhaps had never existed at all anywhere" (p. 303). This is precisely the evidence provided by that brief scene in the ruined mansion.

Actually there has been one other incident prior to this one, which also offered factual corroboration for the Sutpen legend. This is a letter that Mr. Compson produces in which Charles Bon proposes marriage to Judith. It is so fragile with age, so tenuously real, that Quentin can hardly read its "faint spidery script not like something impressed upon the paper by a once-living hand but like a shadow cast upon it which had resolved on the paper the instant before he looked at it and which might fade, vanish, at any instant while he still read . . ." (p. 129).

But even this marginal reality is sufficient to break off the novel's meandering narration and transport us to the climactic moment when Quentin sets off for Sutpen's Hundred with Miss Rosa, there of course to discover Henry Sutpen. The letter thus concludes the first stage of Quentin's involvement with the legend of Thomas Sutpen, the stage in which he is merely a passive listener to what may be merely rumors. The presence of the letter establishes at least that the events Miss Coldfield and his father have told him about existed in some form outside their imaginations. Later, just as writing made the oral legend tangible, the living Henry Sutpen will literally flesh out the shadows haunting Quentin's imagination so that he can nevermore elude them. The quest whose start the real letter had marked, ends with a man who is real enough to die as Quentin emerges from deep within himself (and his heritage) into "the cold air, the iron New England dark" of Cambridge. There he faces the fact that despite everything he still doesn't hate the South—but that he can't go on living with it. Wrenchingly incapable of anything more affirmative, he cries out, " 'I dont. I dont! I dont hate [the South]! I dont hate it!' " (p. 378). Neither does Faulkner: but how to love it? At this moment, the culmination of his most creative period, he can neither go forward, which would mean to abjure at least the aristocratic tradition in Southern history, nor retract the terrible indictment the novel has constituted. After this Faulkner drew back, retreated, never again to expose himself to the terrors that had driven Quentin Compson to suicide.

3

The Ones Named Sambo

Besides Charles Bon, there are a number of other Sutpens in *Absalom, Absalom!* who bear the stigma of black blood. Bon himself has a son with his octoroon mistress who dies when the child, Charles Etienne Saint Valery Bon, is twelve. Thus orphaned (his father has long ago been killed by Henry) the boy is brought to Sutpen's Hundred by Clytie (Clytemnestra) who is herself a black Sutpen, being the daughter of Thomas by a slave. When Etienne Bon dies he too leaves a son corruptedly named Jim Bond, a "hulking, slack-mouthed, saddle-colored" [1] feeble-minded boy who is the last of his line. Everyone else is dead. When they had discovered Henry Sutpen sick in the old mansion, Rosa Coldfield and Quentin had arranged for an ambulance to bring him to the county hospital. However, Clytie, who had hidden and cared for Henry, saw the ambulance coming

[1] *Absalom, Absalom!*, p. 214.

and thought that he was being arrested at last for the murder of Charles Bon. She set fire to the house and died in it along with Henry, thus finally immolating the dream of Thomas Sutpen. The surviving Jim Bond appears something of a perverse victor in a battle between whites and blacks. For as Shreve sums it all up:

"it took Charles Bon and his mother to get rid of old Tom, and Charles Bon and the octoroon to get rid of Judith, and Charles Bon and Clytie to get rid of Henry; and Charles Bon's mother and Charles Bon's grandmother to get rid of Charles Bon. So it takes two niggers to get rid of one Sutpen, don't it?"

Still, even at that rate, he continues, "the Jim Bonds are going to conquer the western hemisphere."

Of course it won't quite be in our time and of course as they spread toward the poles they will bleach out again . . . But it will still be Jim Bond; and so in a few thousand years, I who regard you will also have sprung from the loins of African kings. (p. 378)

Actually, it is not Jim Bond but the Compson's housekeeper in *The Sound the the Fury,* who is usually cited to represent Faulkner's apparent belief that the blacks were the only ones who would survive the decline of the South. But the strength Dilsey emanates amid the Compson cripples, the soundness of her religious faith and of her common sense both, only recall the traditional Mammy virtues Faulkner extolled in his own Mammy, who accepted poverty and overwork "without cavil or calculation or complaint" and thus "earned the gratitude and affection of the family she had conferred the fidelity and devotion upon." [2] Dilsey and her kind will survive because in that oft-quoted pun "they endured." (As one character puts it succinctly, "so [do] mules.") [3] Or, at best, as Faulkner elaborated in later years when he was officially optimistic, Dilsey showed "that the will of man to prevail will even take the nether channel of the black man, the black race, before it will relinquish, succumb, be defeated." [4] What he expected of the coming black ascendancy is explicitly represented in the moronic Jim Bond.

The last of the Compsons is also an idiot, but no one suggests that he and his kind will inherit the earth. On the contrary, in him the Compsons relinquish all future sovereignty, for he represents their final degeneration, their *loss* of self, not their self-realization. Shreve's prediction that "the Jim Bonds" will rule the world implies that they represent blackness at its blackest. There is evidence for this earlier in the novel when Etienne Bon, mortified at learning that he is fractionally black, goes all the way and marries "a coal black and ape-like" mentally retarded woman whom he kennels in a slave cabin on the estate. Etienne himself seems to feel that his wife represents the epitome of his

[2] This admiration of blacks is not uncommon among even the staunchest supporters of the unequal status quo. Thus William Alexander Percy in *Lanterns on the Levee, Recollections of a Planter's Son* remarks that "the farmers, the aristocrats and the Negroes are the only three classes in the South of which God must be proud" (p. 86).

[3] William Faulkner, *Go Down Moses* (New York, 1965), p. 225. McCaslin Edmonds is speaking. And, he continues, dogs share their other virtues of "pity and tolerance and forbearance and fidelity and love of children."

[4] *Faulkner in the University,* p. 5.

despised race, that she manifests with undiluted repulsiveness what is only partial and invisible in him. He "apparently hunt[s] out situations in order to flaunt and fling the ape-like body of his charcoal companion in the faces of all and any who would retaliate," [5] black and white, thus insulting the former and disgusting the latter. One could object that Shreve's racism is his own and that the description of Etienne Bon's wife reflects only Mr. Compson's view. But the Canadian Shreve has nowhere else revealed such attitudes, seeming rather to look upon the whole race issue as another exotic element in Quentin's tale of warmer climes. And Faulkner had already described as a perversity the marriage of a nearly-white man and a very black woman in *Light in August* four years earlier. In his masochistic internalization of Southern values, Joe Christmas also lives with a woman "who resembled an ebony carving." [6] In his depiction of the various black women themselves, in their rank negritude and mute feeble-mindedness, Faulkner clearly indicates the inherent degeneracy of the blackness principle.

Here the issue is race, the inherent character of blacks. (In regard to slavery Faulkner had somewhat more congenial notions, though of dubious origin, which I will take up later.) It is thus, perhaps paradoxically, a literary issue *par excellence* since it has to do directly with the composition of characters. Specifically, whether the blacks of Yoknapatawpha County achieve a more substantial literary form than that contained in the traditional typology is intrinsically an ideological question. The answer lies in the novels and stories comprising the sagas which feature es-

[5] *Absalom, Absalom!*, p. 206.
[6] William Faulkner, *Light in August* (New York, 1950), p. 197.

sentially conventional blacks projecting the racism (the word seems provocative, but there is really no adequate synonym for it) of their author. Moreover, this attitude is implicit throughout Faulkner's opus, indeed remaining remarkably stable despite the other changes evident in his work and the dramatic contemporary social and political developments in the South. The black characters in *The Reivers*, Faulkner's last novel, recall none so much as those in *Soldiers' Pay* and *Sartoris*, while in between the only thing that *The Unvanquished* and *Absalom, Absalom!* have in common (other than their opposition) is their vision of race. It may be in part due to this constancy that Faulkner was able to virtually ignore the issue in the three volumes of the Snopes trilogy which take up the emergence of the New South.

This is not to suggest that Faulkner is merely a latter-day Thomas Nelson Page depicting darkies lacking only servitude to complete their felicity. Yoknapatawpha is full of racial tensions which climax in several lynchings, but these tensions often derive from non-race-connected accidents and anyway yield with suspicious ease to patly moralistic treatment. It is significant, I think, that *Light in August* and *Intruder in the Dust* both conclude calmly after resolving their problems, while *The Sound and the Fury* and *Absalom, Absalom!* end with scenes projecting their own and Faulkner's continuing travail. In short, there is, in the race novels, more dramatizing than drama.

The overlay of Christian mythology on the traditional mulatto tragedy in *Light in August* is a good example of the kind of dramatizing I mean. The relations between the crucifixion of Jesus and the lynching of Joe Christmas are not really functional. We are meant to think about Joe Christmas, whose name refers to the time when he was first found on the steps of an orphanage, as a man who suffers from and perhaps for the sins of white men. But suffering is the only thing he has in common with Christ, for Christmas neither wills his trials nor preaches or even glimpses a better way of life. Being himself quite unaware of the moral issues implicit in his situation, he does not even resemble the Black Christ figure represented notably in Harriet Beecher Stowe's *Uncle Tom*. For although the latter embodies only the meek and not the powerful Jesus, he at least earns the dignity of choosing to endure: he turns his cheek, as it were, while Christmas is slapped around by others. He can be very active at times; and of course he murders Joanna Burden and defies other tormentors. But this has no more to do with the Christ legend than does his passivity: the point is that the hagiography in the novel is finally gratuitous, and in that respect symptomatic of the relative failure of *Light in August* to achieve a coherent inner life.[7]

The problem lies ultimately in Faulkner's very conception of Joe Christmas, whose character, neatly divided along racial lines, can never fuse into a single human being—not even, that is, into one who is torn and schizoid. On the contrary, the two halves of Christmas pull further and further apart until they rip him asunder. Gavin Stevens gives us an account of this fatal moment, which, although hypothetical, is in context highly authoritative. As Stevens

[7] In *Absalom, Absalom!* Faulkner refers to the Old Testament and to Greek tragedy but only for resonance, subsuming everything to the story he himself is telling. Here as in *The Unvanquished* the references to external moralities seem intrusive because where they appear the novel abandons its own identity to them or anyway allows them to dominate.

explains what happened, the mulatto's two bloods flowed in opposite directions.

It (his blood) would not be either one or the other and let his body save itself. Because the black blood drove him first to the Negro cabin. And then the white blood drove him out of there and it was the black blood which snatched up the pistol and the white blood which would not let him fire it. And it was the white blood which sent him to the minister, which rising in him for the last and final time, sent him against all reason and all reality, into the embrace of a chimera, a blind faith in something read in a printed book. Then I believe that the white blood deserted him for the moment. Just a second, a flicker, allowing the black to rise in its final moment and make him turn upon that on which he had postulated his hope of salvation. It was the black blood which swept him by his own desire beyond the aid of any man, swept him up into that ecstasy out of a black jungle where life has already ceased before the heart stops and death is desire and fulfillment. And then the black blood failed him again, as it must have in crises all his life. He did not kill the minister. He merely struck him with the pistol and ran on and crouched behind that overturned table and defied the black blood for the last time, as he had been defying it for thirty years. He crouched behind that table and let them shoot him to death, with that loaded and unfired pistol in his hand.[8]

Leaving aside for the moment the actual events Stevens is describing and the story they culminate, the most striking aspect of this concept of race is that it is totally reified: the two races caged in Joe Christmas constitute real self-contained identities, impossibly yoked together in one body.

[8] *Light in August*, pp. 393–94.

His black blood does not mix with the white but strives to gain control of the single pair of legs and arms, the single head they have to share. Joe Christmas thus exactly recalls Mark Twain's "extraordinary twins" and indeed seems to owe an important debt to all of *Puddn'head Wilson*.

A note appended to Twain's novel explains that it started as a tale about a freakish pair with "two heads and four arms joined to a single body and a single pair of legs" but possessing two distinct identities. One head belonged to a prohibitionist, who unfortunately spent half the week "tight as a brick" from the riotous drinking of the other. The initial plot was to develop the farcical possibilities in this dual personality. The sober twin, for example, although drunk only by proxy, would nearly lose his respectable fiancée. However, as he wrote this story, Mark Twain describes becoming more interested in what had been at first peripheral characters, until he demoted the twins to the supporting cast, separated them, and of their exotic origin retained only the foreign names. There are, in fact, a pair of Italian twins in *Puddn'head Wilson*, but they are especially noted for their likeness and loyalty to one another. Mark Twain seemed to have dropped his original idea of presenting the problem of identity as one of conflicting personalities within a single body.

He had translated it instead from an individual into a social issue. The whole of Dawson's Landing, where *Puddn'head Wilson* is set, is undergoing an identity crisis embodied in a second set of twins with identical appearances but opposite natures. One is black, the other white. The story is well-known: Tom Driscoll and Chambers are born the same day and nursed by the nearly white mother of Chambers, who, fearing that her child will be sold down the river, exchanges the identical babies. The white one grows up a slave and a model of virtue and competence, while the black boy raised for white is in every way corrupt and deficient. At times Mark Twain wonders whether the difference between the two is not due to their divergent nurture. For example, he reports how Tom Driscoll's digestion is ruined by sweets while Chambers grows sturdy on rougher and more wholesome foods. And especially in dealing with Roxanna, the black mother who saves her child the only way she can, the author suggests that circumstances may be more to blame than any innate fault in the criminality of slaves.

But the logic of the construct argues otherwise and finally manifests itself in the ending, when the trick is discovered by Puddn'head Wilson, who has important traits in common with Gavin Stevens. Wilson is also a lawyer, well-educated and ironically affectionate toward his less sophisticated townsfellows. Like Stevens too, Wilson often speaks for the author, and, on balance, this seems to be what he is doing when he steps forward to reveal the truth based on the scientific evidence of the twins' fingerprints taken before and after the exchange. Acting like a prosecutor, Wilson dramatically discloses the proof that Tom Driscoll is a nigger and a murderer or, more precisely, a murdering-nigger. There is a good deal in *Puddn'head Wilson* to qualify the implicit racism of this, of course. Mark Twain explains in his prefatory note that he had slowly become aware that there were two stories in the one he thought to write and one can readily surmise that the question of whether race is to be considered generically or culturally defined underlay his discomfort with a format which began, at least, by assuming the first.

But my concern is with the format itself, the situation of a black man who looks white, as happens in *Light in August* and also in a number of other works, amounting in fact to one traditional way that white writers have depicted blacks. The crucial thing about this genre is that it consistently features blacks who appear white, rather than the other way around. If the author were certain of the equality of his character, it seems more likely that he would project himself into the situation and imagine a white man, whom he knows to be fully human, mistaken for an inferior black. This would be the most telling critique of racism focusing on the way it blinds one race to the essential humanity of others: in white terms, to their whiteness. But Mark Twain, Faulkner, and other writers who have written about mulattos who pass for white only to have their black selves emerge in the end, seem to be making just the opposite point: that even when blacks look equal, i.e., white, they are really black, meaning other, different, and inferior. Finally, the mulatto theme does not speak to the problem of individual identity in a racially divided society, but, quite the contrary, implicitly denies the individualism of its black protagonists. Ralph Ellison's *Invisible Man* makes this point clear by contrast: his novel protests the fact that because the hero is black no one can see him for what he really is. While the lack of definite identity which plagues Joe Christmas represents Faulkner's view that a man cannot know who he is unless he can first identify himself racially.

If having any black blood at all totally taints one's identity, having some white correspondingly improves the character. However, most often this only leads to hopeless aspirations, as depicted in the mixed-blood tragedy, which is just another version of the *Puddn'head Wilson* theme. Two

Southern predecessors of Faulkner, T. S. Stribling and George Washington Cable, wrote tales of this kind and made its implications fully evident. Peter Siner in T. S. Stribling's *Birthright* returns from a Northern education full of zeal for "Negro improvement." Stribling explains Siner's motives just as Gavin Stevens might have:

it was the white blood in his . . . veins that had sent him struggling up North, that had brought him back with this flame in his heart for his own people. It was the white blood in [Siner's fiancée] that kept her struggling to stand up, to speak an unbroken tongue, to gather around her the delicate atmosphere and charm of a gentlewoman. It was the Caucasian in them buried there in Niggertown. It was their part of the tragedy of millions of mixed blood here in the South.[9]

"Perhaps the Negro is not yet capable of more than second-class citizenship," mused Faulkner. "His tragedy may be that so far he is competent for equality only in the ratio of his white blood."[10] Palmyre Philosophe and Honoré Grandissime in Cable's *The Grandissimes* elaborate the same thesis. Honoré is a "free-man coloured" who looks to a stranger from the North exactly like his white cavalier brother. But appearances are once again deceptive, for the black Grandissime ineffectively combines "strong feeling and feeble will (the trait of his caste)." And Palmyre Philosophe, a "magnificent woman" with the "majesty of an empress," is also uncontrollably passionate, quite "untamable."

There is further testimony to black inferiority in such

[9] T. S. Stribling, *Birthright* (New York, 1922), p. 98.
[10] *Faulkner in the University*, p. 210.

characters as Palmyre's maid, a monstrous ebony woman who on one occasion leaps at a visitor, "snarling and gnashing like an ape." In more amiable moods she is seen as a "gibbering black fool." [11] Peter Siner may want to uplift Niggertown but Niggertown is quite jolly in its squalor and promiscuity; in *Light in August* a nursemaid gapes about with "that vacuous idiocy of her idle and illiterate kind" and "in his fumbling and timeless Negro fashion" a messenger loiters while getting the doctor for a dying woman. Entering Mississippi, Joe Christmas meets a black boy shuffling to a lazy, natural rhythm which Christmas can no more follow than he can keep in step with white men. Therein lies his pathos, for lacking certain racial identification Joe Christmas "didn't know what he was, and so he was nothing." Therefore, Faulkner thought, his only salvation in order to live with himself was "to repudiate mankind, to live outside the human race." [12] No wonder, then, if he ended as he did; Faulkner seemed to echo Cable's apostrophe on Palmyre Philosophe, "this monument of the shame of two races," "this poisonous blossom of crime growing out of crime—this final unanswerable white man's accuser—this would-be murderess—what ranks and companies would have to stand up in the Great Day with her and answer as accessory before the fact." [13]

There is a certain irony in Cable's choice of Palmyre as a symbol of white racial crimes, for the very conception that a perverse miscegenation has led to her corruption is

[11] George Washington Cable, *The Grandissimes* (New York, 1920), pp. 174, 263, and 267.

[12] *Faulkner in the University*, p. 72. Faulkner was answering the question: "was he supposed to be part-Negro, or was this supposed to add to the irony of the story?"; p. 118.

[13] *The Grandissimes*, p. 120.

itself profoundly racist. And Cable here expresses the essential view implicit in all the mulatto stories, from *Puddn'head Wilson* to *Light in August*. Slavery and the promiscuous mixing of the races has corrupted Yoknapatawpha as it had Dawson's Landing. So much of the guilt belongs to white men. But, Faulkner seemed quite literally to be saying, that doesn't mean you'd want your sister to marry one.

The relationships between blacks and whites should construct a different kind of family, represented, for example, in the reciprocal caring of Old Simon and the elder Bayard in *Sartoris*. Simon considers himself a Sartoris and scorns the "commonality"; he wears his top hat at a "swaggering tilt" on his "apelike head" and fusses over his "Boss" with all those instincts Faulkner commemorates in Dilsey. But Simon can't really take care of himself, for he is forever getting into debt, whereupon Bayard scolds and threatens but finally bails him out. Simon would be at home in any plantation novel, indeed wishes he might be. He crows with joy at the birth of a male Sartoris, "we gwine wake 'um all up, now. Yessuh, de olden times comin' back ergain, sho'." "Like in Mars' John's time, when de Cunnel wuz de young marster and de niggers fum de quawters gethered on de front lawn, wishin' Mistis en de little marster well." [14] In Faulkner's later writings this idyllic image of the past has considerably faded, but not its desirability. The world of *Light in August* is most lacking in precisely the ability on the part of both races to develop warm familial kinships such as existed between Old Simon and Bayard Sartoris.

Joe Christmas belongs nowhere, he has neither name

[14] *Sartoris*, p. 307.

nor ancestry. The bastard son of a lower-class white woman and a drifter thought to be black but maybe "only" Mexican, he is brought up in an orphanage until the age of five when adopted by Simon McEachern, a farmer who tries to raise the boy into his own harsh, life-denying religion. At the age of seventeen, Joe runs away after a fight with McEachern over a prostitute and wanders the South for fifteen years, challenging both whites and blacks to fight him, each for being alien to themselves, which for the moment yields him a negative but clear identity. Finally, he comes to Yoknapatawpha where he boards with Joanna Burden, the crusading daughter of Northern Calvinists who came South during Reconstruction. (One of her ancestors was killed for a carpetbagger by John Sartoris in *The Unvanquished*.) Christmas and Joanna carry on a perverse affair until the guilt-stricken Joanna has a religious awakening and tries to convert Christmas to it. Christmas slashes her throat with a straight-edged razor and is hunted down, killed, and castrated by a mostly redneck lynch mob led by a fanatic racist named Percy Grimm.

This story has several interesting aspects. The climax of Joe's career is the killing of Joanna Burden, which is so stereotypic an event—the New England old maid "in the wild throes of nymphomania . . . with her wild hair . . . and her wild hands and her breathing: 'Negro! Negro! Negro!' " [15] who reverts to Puritan fanaticism only to be murdered, as any Yoknapatawphan could have predicted, in her bed, by a razor-toting nigger—that one wonders whether it might not be ironically intended to depict racism as a self-fulfilling white concoction. But the context indicates otherwise. Just before the crime, Christmas takes a

[15] *Light in August*, p. 227.

long walk across Jefferson, passing through its black and white communities and thus summarizing his troubled life's journey. At first he walks down the main street of town "like a phantom, a spirit, strayed out of its world, and lost." "Then he found himself. Without his being aware the street had begun to slope and before he knew it he was in Freedman Town, surrounded by the summer smell and the summer voices of invisible Negroes. . . . As from the bottom of a thick black pit he was himself enclosed by cabin shapes." The stress here is on the physical immanence of the ghetto, on its geography and its sounds and smells which identify the race of its inhabitants with inescapable objectivity. Furthermore, since Christmas comes upon racial signs here unaware, we are led to accept the whole concept as real rather than as his own heightened version of a myth.

But the strongest clue we receive to consider black and white as physically rather than culturally distinct is Faulkner's sexual interpretation of each, which, as it were, piles sexism upon racism. Thus in Freedman Town, Christmas finds that "on all sides, even within him, the bodiless fecund-mellow voices of Negro women murmured."

It was as though he and all other man-shaped life about him had been returned to the light-less hot wet primogenitive Female. He began to run . . . and mounted . . . out of the black hollow. He turned . . . running . . . into the higher street. He stopped there, panting, glaring, his heart thudding as if it could or would not yet believe that the air now was the cold hard air of white people.

But he doesn't belong in "the bright quiet of white Jefferson" nor, for that matter, can he be part of Freedman

Town. He had tried to be, earlier, by marrying a black woman.

At night he would lie in bed beside her, sleepless, beginning to breathe deep and hard. He would do it deliberately, feeling, even watching, his white chest arch deeper and deeper within his ribcage, trying to breathe into himself the dark odor, the dark and inscrutable thinking and being of Negroes, with each suspiration trying to expel from himself the white blood and the white thinking and being. And all the while his nostrils at the odor which he was trying to make his own would whiten and tauten, his whole being writhe and strain with physical outrage and spiritual denial.[16]

Again racial character is a matter of physiology, and only secondarily psychological and cultural. Joe Christmas is like Honoré Grandissime and Peter Siner, neither one nor the other, neither here nor there, and therefore nowhere. (Among the human equivalents of asses and horses, there seems to be no place for mules.) And that Christmas cannot even be certain that he bears the fatal spot represents an ultimate stage in the erosion of the old ground on which Simon and Sartoris both stood firmly.

Let me repeat. The issue in *Light in August* is not whether or not its author was racist. The issue is how his thinking and feeling about matters of race helped form his novel. I am suggesting here that Faulkner's ultimate inability to believe in the intrinsic equality of blacks, while nonetheless opposing their unequal social treatment, split the very form of *Light in August* into two conflicting parts. Easily the most successful, the most significant and interesting is the part which tells the tragic story of the crushing of Joe

[16] *Light in August*, pp. 99–100, 197.

Christmas between two antithetical social beings contending within him. But, like its hero, the novel also harbors an
antithetical other self. That self, which finally degenerates
to the level of Gavin Stevens's silly last speech, wants to
argue that race itself is the problem, that one must be either black or white because these are inherently incom-
mensurate identities.

Had the novel been focussed on a white character
beset by these conflicting views, Faulkner's participation in
the conflict need not have been a problem. Indeed, like
Sutpen, such a character might have tapped the energy that
contradictory views generate, and transformed it into a
complex vitality. In Hightower, Faulkner briefly begins to
achieve this. But his central character is really Joe Christmas, for whom the author's uncertainty about the human
potential of blacks, and, specifically, their potential as a
novel's focal consciousness, proves ultimately fatal. Remaining an Other in his own fictional world, Christmas can
never become fully its Subject. The fact that the Stevens
speech does not totally shatter the coherence of the novel
as a whole means that the novel as a whole suffers from in-
coherence.

Another suggestive facet of the Christmas story is its
constituency of nearly all lower-class whites, or anyway
plain folk. Gavin Stevens enters the scene only after the
death of Christmas, who, in all his odyssey, never meets
any of the nobility who people most of the early writings,
and who are always assumed to be the apex of Yoknapatawpha society. The absence of aristocrats here has the essential effect of absolving them of guilt in the fate of Christmas, and, more importantly, absolving with them the
traditional forms of Southern society as a whole. We are

never aware in connection with the trials of Joe Christmas of Yoknapatawpha's social structure or of any group as such within it, with the partial exception of the church.[17] Not even the rednecks are accused, despite the existence of some stereotypic racists among them, for others are clearly decent people with only the rustic conservatism one expects in farmers. What civil authority there is lines up on the side of virtue when the sheriff does his best to prevent the lynching. Most of the community is with him; even those who follow Grimm are shocked by his violation of the body, and will, Faulkner predicts, remember the incident "in whatever peaceful valleys, beside whatever placid and reassuring streams of old age" where they may ever after dwell. Which is just the point: that the universe in which Joe Christmas leads his devastated life also contains peaceful valleys and the promise of a secure old age. And in that larger universe even the memory of having participated in the killing of Joe Christmas can be ultimately superseded by life itself, by a second chance.

This hope was totally lacking in *The Sound and the Fury,* and when Quentin Compson realized that the past had swallowed up the future, he committed suicide; it was lacking again four years later in *Absalom, Absalom!* where Quentin came to feel "older at twenty than a lot of people who have died." The hopefulness of *Light in August* reflects Faulkner's sense that the doom which had overtaken the Old South resulted not from racial crimes, which in themselves constituted sad but redeemable excesses, but from a fundamental misordering of white society.[18]

[17] See later discussion of the Reverend Gail Hightower.
[18] This point is developed in Chapter IV through the discussion of *Go Down Moses.*

When he focused on race as an isolated problem he did not despair. Quite the contrary, as the structure of *Light in August* indicates. The novel opens and closes not with Christmas but with the inspiring tale of Lena Grove, who also wanders the South but who is never lost. Seven months pregnant, Lena has set out in search of her lover who has abandoned her but whom she confidently expects to find waiting for her in their new home. " 'I reckon a family ought to all be together when a chap comes . . . I reckon the Lord will see to that.' " Her travels contrast in every way with those of Christmas as the people on her way treat her with a compassion that triumphs easily over their religious bigotry. She not only comes through the violence of the novel unscathed, but redeems the lives of others. Her story frames and subsumes that of Christmas; there is even a suggestion that her son, born just as Christmas dies, represents his rebirth: certainly it signifies that in *Light in August* life is stronger than death.

But the victory means little, for Lena Grove in no way speaks to the issues embodied in Christmas. She represents only an abstract affirmation, an allegory in which a spirit of the life-giving earth passes through a scene of death and destruction and causes the flowers to bloom once more. In fact, by this allegorical cast she highlights another device besides the Christian mythological references, by which Faulkner tries to infuse substance or acceptable meanings into a novel whose real theme he treats with some diffidence. He was asked once about the emblematic names of the characters—besides Joe Christmas, there is Gail Hightower, the dreaming irresponsible priest, Calvin Burden, the Northern fanatic with a mission to save black souls, and, of course, Percy Grimm—and explained that it came from "my memory of the old miracle plays . . . in early English literature." [19] Lena too recalls a literature of abstract truths even to her journey, which she pursues with the fine confidence of those heroes who never doubted that they would shortly find dragon, grail, or Camelot.

Never really a wasteland, despite Christmas, Yoknapa-tawpha is further improved by her visit, and when she leaves, something of her inspiration remains behind embodied especially in the revived conscience of the town's lapsed priest. Gail Hightower is the only white man of good family in the novel and his role does temporarily qualify but ultimately confirms the racial probity of his class. His were sins of omission, rather more easily redeemed than those of Sutpen or even Sartoris. The comparison is apt, for the story of Hightower is another version of the cavalier recalling plot, leading here to a conclusion that accords with Faulkner's differing valuations of problems of race and class. Hightower is an old recluse who was once minister of a Jefferson congregation but was expelled for failure to discharge his duties and, it seemed to the good people, general craziness. The method in this madness was that familiar constant obsession with the past, which possesses so many of Faulkner's gentlemen. Like them too, Hightower dwells on a particular incident which, in fact, recalls almost exactly the confederate Bayard's escapade in *Sartoris*.

In the last year of the Civil War, Hightower's grandfather led a small band of rebels into occupied Jefferson to burn the Yankee army's stores. At the head of his men, Hightower galloped down the main street in broad daylight past hundreds of astonished Yankee troops in "a prank so foolhardy that the troops who had opposed them for four

[19] *Faulkner in the University*, p. 97.

years did not believe that even they would have attempted
it." But like Jeb Stuart's gallant band, Hightower's succeeds
in its mission and escapes. Then, "with all that for background, backdrop: the consternation, the conflagration,"
mostly to dramatize their defiance of normal caution they
raid a chicken-coop. Naturally Hightower is killed. "They
didn't know who fired the shot. . . . It may have been a
woman, likely enough the wife of a Confederate soldier."
The Reverend Hightower hopes it was: "it's fine so. Any
soldier can be killed by the enemy in the heat of battle.
. . . But with a shotgun, a fowling piece, in a henhouse
. . ." It is its incongruity, the wastefulness of his grandfather's death, which epitomizes for Gail Hightower the vanished cavalier era. Even Miss Jenny's admiration in *Sartoris*
for the gratuitous gallantry of Confederate officers did not
thus depend on its usefulness. The past is here ephemeral,
without real substance; the tragedy of the Old South, as
Faulkner saw it elsewhere, has shrunk into an old man's
daydream of "the wild bugles and the clashing sabres and
the wild thunder of hooves." [20]

Had Faulkner, then, facing contemporary problems of
race, abandoned the old ways and his dashing aristocrats?
Not at all. For by reducing the importance of the past as he
does here, he evades the issues raised in other versions
and escapes their conclusion, as it emerges in *Absalom,
Absalom!*, that forces out of Southern history have structured Yoknapatawpha County in ways that merely abstract
moralizing cannot reform. In short, in *Light in August*, the
structure of past society escapes analysis as readily as does
the present system. Solutions come correspondingly easier
too. Hightower has yielded to his obsession with his grand-

[20] *Light in August,* pp. 423, 425, and 432.

father's death to the point of neglecting his own life and the lives of his flock. The church seemed to him only a refuge from living where he could commune with the dead, and that was wrong, as he comes to realize when Lena, as life-force, jars him awake. When he helps deliver her baby, he is himself reborn, whereupon he assumes his responsibilities as a minister and spiritual leader, and moments later tries, albeit too late, to shield Joe Christmas from the pursuing mob.

In this context, even the agony of Christmas becomes life-giving and, informed by Christian associations, blends without too much difficulty into the novel's remarkably optimistic ending. It is true that Hightower dies shortly but he has now lived and seen the truth. More importantly, the lesson he has learned survives to provide a peaceful conclusion to the discordant tale of Joe Christmas. When *Light in August* ends, Jefferson seems morally viable, although its racial attitudes have not changed at all.

The violent implementation of these attitudes is clearly repugnant, but it can probably be prevented in the future by men like the Reverend Hightower who have to forget the past and exert leadership now. Good whites must be responsible not only for blacks, but for less favored whites as well. Sixteen years later, *Intruder in the Dust* (1948) would provide the definitive statement of this principle embodied in Charles Mallison, who bravely shoulders the white gentleman's burden.

4

They Endured

But before Charles Mallison grew up to open a new era of white moderation, Faulkner wrote *Go Down Moses* (1942), his most searching, most artistically effective treatment of race. This is a collection of stories about the McCaslin-Edmonds family of planters and their slaves, later their sharecroppers, the Beauchamps. Blacks and whites are intricately bound together by a series of sometimes incestuous relationships reaching back to Carothers McCaslin (1772–1837), who bought the land from the Chickasaw chieftain, Ikkemotubbe (who also sold the Compsons their land). "Was," the first story, takes place before the War, and the others span the period down to the eve of the book's appearance. It is dedicated to "Mammy,"

Caroline Barr
Who was born in Slavery and
who gave to my family a fidelity

without stint or calculation of
recompense and to my childhood
an immeasurable devotion
and love.

But the Mammy in these stories, Molly Beauchamp, with
her clean white "headrag" and apron, is overshadowed by
a less complaisant husband, Lucas Beauchamp, "the oldest
McCaslin descendant still living on the land even though in
the world's eye he descended not from McCaslins but from
McCaslin slaves." [1] His blackness is in no way feminine
(neither in the Dilsey sense nor in that of *Light in August*);
Lucas Beauchamp is the proud grandson of Carothers Mc-
Caslin himself and thus, as he likes to say, a "man-made"
McCaslin, unlike the current owner of the plantation who,
being an Edmonds, is a McCaslin only on his mother's side.
The white McCaslin line ends with Isaac (Ike), who repudi-
ates his heritage and abandons the plantation. Since Ike
has no children, the last McCaslin will be the great-grand-
nephew of Lucas, a Jim Bond as it were, but one whom
Faulkner seems here willing to recognize as legitimate. Although we see this black McCaslin only as a baby, we do
know that he is neither deformed nor mentally retarded
and that his mother, raised in the North, might readily pass
for white.

Indeed she almost does and in the process shocks Ike
McCaslin into revealing that he may have renounced his
plantation but yet retains something of the planter outlook.
A well-spoken, comely young woman arrives at the hunting
camp one day looking for Carothers Edmonds, the father of
her child. Only after awhile does Ike in "amazement, pity

[1] *Go Down Moses*, pp. 33–34.

and outrage" realize " 'You're a nigger!' " But then he cries out against the very thought that they might marry: *"Maybe in a thousand or two thousand years in America,* he thought, *But not now!"* It is clear in context that Faulkner does not endorse Ike's revulsion. For when, horrified, he urges that she go back North at once and marry "a man in your own race. That's the only salvation for you—for a while yet, maybe a long while yet," it is the woman who has the last word: " 'Old man,' she said, 'have you lived so long and forgotten so much that you don't remember anything you ever knew or felt or even heard about love?' " [2] The story thus establishes control over Ike's racism and projects a larger tolerance.

There is further evidence in *Go Down Moses* that Faulkner had somehow extricated his extraordinary imagination from racial attitudes which previously (and again later) bound it to stereotypes. One of the stories in the collection, "Pantaloon in Black," is explicitly critical of white men who refuse to recognize the common humanity of a black. A "pantaloon," of course, is a masked dramatic character, generally a buffoon. The story's image is thus essentially the same as Ellison's and inverts the conception of *Light in August,* by pointing to an internal man, hidden from whites by his black skin. The man is named Rider. He is a hero, bigger, stronger, braver, and harder-working than his fellow millhands but tragically flawed by the "vanity of his own strength," which leads him to defy God and, incidentally, the white man. When his young wife dies, Rider refuses to endure his loss quietly as his relatives advise: " 'De Lawd guv, and He tuck away . . . Put yo faith

---

[2] "Delta Autumn," *Go Down Moses,* p. 272, and pp. 274–75.

and trust in him.' " He demands explanations; " 'Whut faith and trust?' " he wants to know. " 'Whut Mannie ever done ter Him? Whut he wanter come messin wid me?' " Wandering about dazed with sorrow after the funeral of his wife, Rider gets into a dice game with a redneck named Birdsong, who, as everyone around knows, " 'has been running crooked dice on them mill niggers for fifteen years.' " This time Rider challenges the loaded dice and Birdsong pulls out a pistol, but the black hero is stronger and kills him. The Birdsongs take their revenge: "they found [Rider] on the following day, hanging from the bell-rope in a negro schoolhouse about two miles from the saw-mill."

Faulkner tells the story in two sections. The first, narrated by a neutrally omniscient voice whose account we therefore consider true, describes the sudden disintegration of Rider's life after six months of idyllic marriage, in a cabin whose "rent was paid promptly in advance,"

and even in just six months he had refloored the porch and rebuilt and roofed the kitchen doing the work himself on Saturday afternoon and Sunday with his wife helping him, and bought the stove. Because he made good money: saw-milling ever since he began to get his growth at fifteen and sixteen and now, at twenty-four, head of the timber gang itself because the gang he headed moved a third again as much timber between sunup and sundown as any other moved . . . (pp. 108–09)

This is a very different set of virtues from the ones Faulkner elsewhere associated with black characters; Rider is defined in and by action, as a man aggressively creating his own world, moreover through the hallowed means of manual labor. His story constitutes a sort of classical tragedy in which a heroic figure, unwilling to accept the confines of mortality, dies rather than surrender his honor. But the tensions of the hero's struggle to transcend mere humanity are tremendously heightened here by the restricted ground on which Rider, because of his subhuman social status, must remain. It is as if Hamlet had to play out his torment in a cage at the zoo.

Or, as the deputy sheriff who finds Rider's body explains it, " 'Them damn niggers,

"I swear to godfrey, it's a wonder we have as little trouble with them as we do. Because why? Because they aint human. They look like a man and they walk on their hind legs like a man, and they can talk and you can understand them and you think they are understanding you, at least now and then. But when it comes to the normal human feelings and sentiments of human beings, they might just as well be a damn herd of wild buffaloes." (pp. 121–22)

This deputy narrates the second part of the story in a long monologue to a wife impatient to get out to the movies. In the deputy's version, Rider's frantic behavior at the burial becomes an unashamed eagerness to "rush her into the ground," and all subsequent departures from black conventions—meaning loud but resigned grieving—prove Rider's nonhumanity. But the story's commitment to an opposite view is so strong that at times the deputy's account recalls a Browning monologue. He is the one, for instance, to report Rider's last words without realizing their import: " 'Hit look lack Ah just cant quit thinking. Look lack Ah just cant quit' " (p. 125).[3] And when Rider confesses and promises not to escape if only the lawmen don't lock him up

[3] "Pantaloon in Black," *Go Down Moses*, pp. 114, 123, 121, 108–09, 121–22, 125.

alone with his torment, the white man gives up trying to understand anyone so alien to the human race. The achievement of Rider is the more impressive in that, unlike Joe Christmas, he is wholly black, a giant with strong ties to his community and culture, an antithesis therefore to Dilsey or Simon.

But for most of *Go Down Moses,* the dedication to Mammy turns out to be appropriate after all; "Pantaloon in Black" is a minor episode in the collection and essentially unrelated to its ongoing plot. Rider appears nowhere else in this or any other of Faulkner's work; the intense imaginative effort evident in *Go Down Moses* had apparently thrown him off as a spark, an adumbration of a racial thesis not really in accord with that of the book as a whole. For, in context, Faulkner's criticism of Ike has less to do with the ideology of enforced segregation than with its practicality. The story in which Ike encounters the black-white woman is entitled "Delta Autumn," and depicts the last of the annual hunts conducted by a group of Yoknapatawpha planters, passing the tradition from father to son, since before the Civil War. Their forays into the wilderness were a ritual, welding anew each year an important accord between nature and the cavalier code. Now the wilderness has all but disappeared, and the last McCaslin cavalier is the Carothers Edmonds whose only son is black. No new dawn is forecast in that baby, but a darkening twilight which Faulkner sees represented as surely by the child's impure blood as by the pollution of the land. If Faulkner disagrees with Ike's die-hard response to it, he shares the old man's vision of the New South: "This Delta, he thought: this Delta."

This land which man has deswamped and denuded and derivered in two generations so that white men can own plantations and commute every night to Memphis and black men own plantations and ride in jim crow cars to Chicago to live in millionaires' mansions on Lakeshore Drive, where white men rent farms and live like niggers and niggers crop on shares and live like animals, where cotton is planted and grows man-tall in the very cracks of the sidewalks, and usury and mortgage and bankruptcy and measureless wealth, Chinese and African and Aryan and Jew, all breed and spawn together until no man has time to say which one is which nor cares. . . .[4]

But what is most interesting about the babel of races which has come to punish man's arrogant misuse of the land ("No wonder the ruined woods I used to know don't cry for retribution! Ike thought: The people who have destroyed it [sic] will accomplish its revenge"—p. 275) is its pervasive democracy. There are rich whites and poor whites, as there are rich blacks and poor. The idea that blacks and whites lead equally problematical lives in a confused society appears in many guises throughout the stories. Thus Faulkner describes as a "paradox" the relationship between Lucas Beauchamp and McCaslin Edmonds, who are coevals on the family tree: "old Cass a McCaslin only on his mother's side and so bearing his father's name though he possessed the land and its benefits and responsibilities; Lucas a McCaslin on his father's side though bearing his mother's name and possessing the use and benefit of the land with no responsibilities."[5] Indeed by a poetic process the paradox renders "the analogy [be-

[4] "Delta Autumn," p. 275.   [5] *Go Down Moses,* p. 40.

tween them] only the closer." And this is finally the central theme of *Go Down Moses,* that blacks and whites in the South are of one family brought together by their very divisions.

In the 1930's Dilsey grew restive under Mrs. Compson's sarcasm. In response *Go Down Moses* projects a new rationale for a voluntary segregation which in its new form would be better called separateness. Anyway, Faulkner argues, not unlike the old-time planters, since underneath it all the South is all one family, like the McCaslins-Edmonds, the separateness is only temporary; sometime in the future, perhaps not as far as Ike's two thousand years but certainly "not now," the races would spontaneously integrate not to conform with laws but in expression of an underlying integration which had anyway always prevailed.

Lucas Beauchamp is the perfect embodiment of this concept. He stands proudly apart from the whites to whom if anything he considers himself superior. With a dubious jocularity, Faulkner half agrees with him, as when he suggests that an Edmonds is a "lesser man" than Lucas, "since it was not Lucas who paid taxes, insurance, and interest or owned anything which had to be kept ditched, drained, fenced, and fertilized or gambled anything save his sweat, and that only as he saw fit, against God for his yearly sustenance." [6]

And Beauchamp is pointedly at his very best insisting on a segregation that his white cousins would perhaps

[6] *Go Down Moses,* p. 52. Quentin's quip about Deacon, an old black hanger-on at Harvard, that because of Quentin's slaveowning grandfather Deacon "can spend day after day marching in parades. If it hadn't been for my grandfather, he'd have to work like whitefolks" (*The Sound and the Fury,* p. 69), is further evidence of the continuity in Faulkner's thinking about blacks.

breach. Thus in "The Fire and the Hearth" Lucas and his son accept Carothers Edmonds' claim to deferential treatment with such alacrity that he realizes too late that they have segregated him rather than he them. Much of the strength of the young woman who faced down Ike McCaslin in "Delta Autumn" had indeed flowed from her prior decision to let her white lover go and to marry, if anyone, a black man. The notion of a separate equality, of course, retains intact the reified definition of race in *Light in August*. If Lucas has achieved control over his two racial identities, this does not at all mean that they have reconciled, much less fused. Faulkner seems not to consider that event a possibility and his description of Lucas' handling of the mixed blood dilemma is finally only a variant of the Joe Christmas tragedy:

It was as if [Lucas] were not only impervious to [his white] blood, he was indifferent to it. He didn't even need to strive with it. He didn't even have to bother to defy it. He resisted it simply by being the composite of the two races which made him, simply by possessing it. Instead of being at once the battle-ground and victim of the two strains, he was a vessel, durable, ancestryless, non-conductive, in which the toxin and its anti stalemated one another, seetheless, unrumoured in the outside air.[7]

Predictably, the implication of black inferiority which underlies this notion of two bloods (historically, if not logically) is there even in episodes which ostensibly celebrate Lucas but disparage his black side.

One such is the confrontation between Lucas and Zack Edmonds that occurs in "The Fire and the Hearth." Lucas

[7] *Go Down Moses*, p. 86.

does come off the winner, it is true, and this is the more significant in that their dispute concerns the vexed issue of sexual relations between master and slave (in this case, landowner and tenant) which had yielded the abolitionists some of their most persuasive arguments. (The immediate spur to Ike's repudiation of his inheritance had indeed been the discovery that his grandfather had had an incestuous affair with his own slave daughter.) Lucas' ordeal begins when Zack's wife dies in childbirth and he moves Molly into the big house, to nurse the infant and be his housekeeper. Although Zack swears that she has no more illicit duties, Lucas demands her return. " 'I want my wife. I needs her at home . . . I wants her in my house tonight. You understand?' " Nor does her eventual discharge really avenge Lucas' honor. " *'I will have to kill him,'* " he thinks, " *'or I will have to take her and go away.'* " So he confronts Edmonds, saying, " 'You thought that because I am a nigger I wouldn't even mind,' " shoots at him, and the gun misfires. Here the episode ends, with Beauchamp having vindicated his manhood and fate having preserved the life of Zack. Still, Lucas Beauchamp wonders, " 'How to God can a black man ask a white man to please not lay down with his black wife? And even if he could ask it, how to God can the white man promise he wont?' " [8] For a moment, their social inequality so glaringly revealed, the two men seem to face each other as equals.

But the situation veers away from this; even as Lucas defines his plight in black terms, we are constantly reminded that he is himself part white. He in fact attributes his courage to the blood of old Carothers McCaslin; facing Edmonds and preparing to kill him, Lucas tells the white

[8] "The Fire and the Hearth," *Go Down Moses,* pp. 42 and 43.

man that he should have expected this when he took Molly. " 'You knowed I wasn't afraid, because you knowed I was a McCaslin too and a man-made one.' " And later, when Zack is fortuitously saved, Lucas realizes that he too has escaped because "*I would have paid. I would have waited for the rope, even the coal oil. I would have paid. So I reckon I aint got old Carothers' blood for nothing, after all.*" This recalls exactly Joe Christmas prevented by his white blood from fighting those who are lynching him for a nigger. In fact, despite that inner stalemate, Lucas quite often resembles those mulattos of Faulkner's earlier writings. His features are "Syriac," and once when Ike looks at Lucas he sees "the composite tintype face of ten thousand undefeated Confederate soldiers" despising him for having "*reneged, cried calf-rope, sold my birthright, betrayed my blood*" (pp. 46, 51, 89). It is a tortuous process by which a black man comes to look most like a Confederate soldier and to despise the son of slaveowners for renouncing his heritage. But it is Faulkner's conception of how the South has achieved genuine integration. Ike reflects that black Lucas Beauchamp is

more like Carothers than all the rest of us put together, including old Carothers. He is both heir and prototype simultaneously of all the geography and climate and biology which sired old Carothers and all the rest of us and our kind, myriad, countless, faceless, even nameless now except himself who fathered himself, intact and complete, contemptuous, as old Carothers must have been, of all blood black white yellow or red, including his own. (p. 96)

Thus Lucas at times comes to define the single race of Southerners. For him personally this is ambiguous enough to allow considerable character development and occasionally to allow the emergence of trans-racial emotions and experiences. But the aspects of universal manhood proclaimed in Lucas are always defined in white, indeed upper-class white, terms: Lucas transcends blackness but not whiteness, of which an exalted version is in fact the ideal.

Nor does the fact that a white Edmonds is not as good as a McCaslin really qualify the value of white blood *per se*. After all, certain whites are better than others; Lucas looks down on the sheriff, "a redneck without any reason for pride in his forbears nor hope for it in his descendants" (p. 39). But all are to be measured by the standard of the cavalier culture. The best white man is the founder of the book's microcosmic society, Carothers McCaslin, and the others range themselves on a scale descending from him. If certain blacks are whiter than some whites, this only demonstrates that there really are two distinct kinds of beings but that their proximity has generated hybrid individuals. We are back on familiar ground.

And Lucas himself constantly reverts to type. For instance, immediately following Ike's recognition in him of transcendent Southern Man, Lucas visits Zack Edmonds to ask him to arrange for a "voce" between him and Aunt Molly. Lucas is sixty-seven and his wife only a year or two younger, so bent and frail that she seems smaller than a ten-year-old child. But she is determined to divorce Lucas because she can no longer put up with his latest nonsense, hunting for buried gold all night every night, with a divining machine brought from Memphis. The situation is quaintly comic and might have made a skit in a minstrel show. Edmonds scolds everyone but recognizes that it is his responsibility to shoo them back to their senses; with much aggravation for the white man, it all comes right in the end. Except that Lucas has turned irrevocably into a nigger. Faulkner tries to revive him by invoking his better self: as the episode ends Edmonds watches Lucas in the distance, "erect beneath the old, fine well-cared-for hat, walking with that unswerving and dignified deliberation which every now and then, and with something sharp at the heart, Edmonds recognized as having come from his own ancestry too as the hat had come" (p. 105).

But Lucas' white ancestry seems incongruous here where we see him acting rather like a lovable old darky, and it is difficult to believe that Edmonds feels anything sharper at his heart than parental exasperation.

This is not an isolated instance in *Go Down Moses.* Indeed episodes like this form the substance of most of the stories, comprising a context which seriously qualifies such better moments as the confrontation of Lucas and Edmonds over Molly. Moreover, even this confrontation, occurring in "The Fire and the Hearth," is set within devaluating parentheses. The story closes with the divorce incident just described and opens with an episode that is similarly demeaning. It seems that Lucas has been making illegal whiskey on the plantation for over twenty years; now his future son-in-law George Wilkins is threatening the operation by setting up his own still so indiscreetly that the authorities are sure to be alerted. Lucas has decided, therefore, to turn Wilkins in to Edmonds who will send him to the State Penitentiary and thus unwittingly allow Lucas to conduct his business in peace. One readily visualizes the shuffle, as the old man, muttering to himself, sets about this complicated plot. Naturally it all goes awry and Edmonds has to set things right. At times like these Lucas seems a first cousin to Simon, Bayard Sartoris' lovable old nemesis.

The emphasis on kinship between blacks and whites in *Go Down Moses* is thus revealed originating in the old claim that the plantation was one harmonious and inter-dependent family. Within the family, Lucas can be proud and independent, but one wonders how he would do on his own. One indication may be that his sister, Fonsiba, nearly goes under when she leaves home and has to be rescued by a white McCaslin. Foolish Fonsiba runs off with a romantic stranger. Some months later Ike, seeking her out to deliver a legacy of one thousand dollars which Carothers McCaslin has left to all his black progeny, finds her on a farm in Arkansas, nearly starved in a "draughty, damp, heatless, negro-stale negro-rank sorry room" while her husband in a frock coat sits reading a book through "lensless spectacles" and spinning grandiose plans for a mythical spring, meanwhile living off the pension his father earned by fighting in the Yankee army (pp. 212–14). Ike ensures Fonsiba's minimum sustenance by arranging to have the monthly interest from the legacy delivered directly to her so that her husband cannot squander it on tokens of spurious equality. The episode speaks for itself, even to the nice touch of having her only dependable income and security come from an ancestral slavemaster.

But Faulkner is not merely venting contempt for uppity niggers. There is another dimension to the story which emerges through an argument between Ike and Fonsiba's "scholar-husband" over the meaning of emancipation. Holding his book in a "workless hand," the black man speaks "his measured and sonorous imbecility of the boundless folly and the baseless hope" that "The curse you whites brought into this land has been lifted. . . . We are seeing a new era, an era dedicated, as our founders intended it, to freedom, liberty, and equality for all, to which this country will be the new Canaan." Appalled, Ike punctures this rhetoric, asking "Freedom from what? From work?" and cries out,

"Dont you see? This whole land, the whole South, is cursed, and all of us who derive from it, whom it ever suckled, white and black both, lie under the curse? Granted that my people brought the curse on to the land: maybe for that reason their descendants alone can—not resist it, not combat it—maybe just endure and outlast it until the curse is lifted. Then your people's turn will come because we have forfeited ours. But not now. Not yet. Dont you see?" (p. 212)

As Ike reads Southern history (one critic considers him the first of Faulkner's characters to understand history),[9] it has from the first violated the dictates of both God and nature: nature is there to sustain man but it should not therefore be polluted; blacks are lesser beings than whites but should not have been enslaved. Invoking the American belief that the new country constituted a new world, Ike associates private ownership of land and slavery as twin abuses inherited from the old world to defile the new, which thus incurred a second fall. But Ike seems to suggest that there was something fortunate about this fall as about the first, for it has afforded sinners the chance of a better salvation.

Certainly his assumption of guilt is not all abnegation. Trying to explain to his cousin Edmonds why he has de-

[9] R. W. B. Lewis, *The American Adam* (Chicago, 1968), p. 197.

cided to "relinquish and repudiate" his estate and live instead the humble life of a carpenter, Ike speculates that he may be the blessed if tormented instrument of God's will to use "the blood which he had brought in the evil to destroy the evil" (p. 198). The Civil War especially seems credible to Ike only as divinely inspired madness, fomented by God when he concluded that *"Apparently they can learn nothing save through suffering, remember nothing save when underlined in blood."* In short, with divine irony, God sent the slavemasters "to set at least some of His lowly people free." Meanwhile the lowly will be bound "for a while yet, a little while yet." "Through and beyond that life and maybe through and beyond the life of that life's sons and maybe even through and beyond that of the sons of those sons. But not always, because they will endure" (pp. 218, 198, 224).

This is what Ike tries to explain to Sophonsiba's husband, who, in arguing that the abolition of slavery has "voided and discharged" the curse upon the South, is not proposing reconciliation but the end of white rule. But in Ike's conception, ratified by his voluntary expiation, the white man's burden has become a Christian trial. There is an interesting contrast here to Harriet Beecher Stowe's image of a black Christ essentially bearing a black man's burden. God has chosen to crucify specifically the white man: it is his torment, but also his pride. For a little later, in one of those marvelously ordered monologues consisting of an unbroken sentence running several pages but maintaining its organic coherence throughout, Ike significantly qualifies his conception of whites as guilty instruments of God's will. He now reflects that, if the divine purpose was to drown in blood the evil which a flood of waters had failed to expunge, only the cavalier could have served. "Who else could have declared a war against a power with ten times the area and a hundred times the men and a thousand times the resources, except men who could believe that all that was necessary to conduct a successful war was not acumen nor shrewdness nor politics nor diplomacy nor money or even integrity and simple arithmetic but just love of land and courage" (p. 220). Considered in this frame of mind, even slavery had its points. After all, the wives and daughters of the planters "made soups and jellies for them when they were sick and carried the trays through the mud and the winter too into the stinking cabins and sat in the stinking cabins and kept fires going until crises came and passed . . . which the white man would have done too for any other of his cattle that was sick but at least the man who hired one from a livery wouldn't have" (p. 218). Ike has here become an apologist making the familiar argument that slaves were better off than wage workers because the masters felt responsible for their slaves and had an economic interest in keeping them fit.

His agonized repudiation of his heritage thus encompasses a contradictory reaffirmation of two important claims of the plantation myth, that the cavalier excelled in courage and dedication and that slaves were relatively well off in the parental care of their owners. But there is perhaps little opposition between the repudiation and the affirmation, which meet on the common ground of Ike's belief in white superiority. That granted, it can readily be both a proud and a shameful thing to be a white man, as it is both to be human. We kill each other, it is true, but we are better than monkeys.

What is more, Ike's very abnegation has been in part forecast by his ancestors who were also men of conscience. His father and uncle (twin sons of Carothers McCaslin named Buck and Buddy) had already discharged some of the family guilt by freeing their slaves. In fact, their attitude to the land, the belief that the land did not belong to men but men to the land, was closely related to Ike's later attitude. *Go Down Moses* begins in the time of Buck and Buddy with a story called "Was," which still further exculpates the McCaslins by depicting their plantation, as a convivial overgrown farm, a place where even slavery was fun. "Was" tells the story of Tomey's Turl, the son of Carothers McCaslin by his own (slave) daughter, who regularly runs away to the neighboring plantation to visit his slave fiancée, Tennie. Each time he does, Uncle Buck saddles up and gives chase with his dogs. Turl's incestuous origin only accentuates the closeness of the McCaslin clan here, while the slave hunt, Stowe's most memorable image to connote the horrors of slavery, has become an occasion for slapstick that everyone can enjoy, perhaps especially the slave who in the end wins out by forcing the McCaslins to buy Tennie in order to keep him safely at home.

Several elements contribute to the coziness of an episode which could as well have been macabre. The humorous repetition of Turl's unsuccessful flights prevents our taking any one of them very seriously, and our detachment is further encouraged by the animal simile through which Faulkner describes the whole affair. The discovery that Tomey's Turl "has run again" coincides this time with the escape of a tame fox whom the dogs chase with great noise and confusion.

When [Ike] and Uncle Buck ran back to the house from dis-
covering that Tomey's Turl had run again, they heard Uncle
Buddy cursing and bellowing in the kitchen, then the fox
and the dogs came out of the kitchen and crossed the hall
into the dogs' room and they heard them run through the
dogs' room and . . . into the kitchen again and this time it
sounded like the whole kitchen chimney had come down
and Uncle Buddy bellowing like a steamboat blowing and
this time the fox and the dogs and five or six sticks of
firewood all came out of the kitchen together with Uncle
Buddy in the middle of them hitting at everything in sight
with another stick. It was a good race. (p. 10)

The fox eludes the dogs until Uncle Buck puts him back in
his cage. When moments later the quarry becomes Tomey's Turl the situation is the same:

he never did know just when and where they jumped Tomey's Turl, whether he flushed out of one of the cabins or
not. . . . Uncle Buck roared, . . . "I godfrey, he broke
cover . . ." and Black John's [the horse] feet clapped four
times like pistol shots . . . then he and Uncle Buck vanished over the hill . . . "Cast [the dogs]!" and they all
piled over the crest of the hill just in time to see Tomey's
Turl away out across the flat, almost to the woods, and the
dogs streaking down the hill and out on to the flat. They
just tongued once and when they came boiling up around
Tomey's Turl it looked like they were trying to jump up and
lick him in the face until even Tomey's Turl slowed down
and he and the dogs all went into the woods together. . . .
It wasn't any race at all. (pp. 18–19)

Uncle Buck remains hopeful (" 'I godfrey,' " he says later.
" 'We've got him. . . . He's going to earth. We'll cut back

to the house and head him before he can den' "—p. 20)
but to no avail. Eventually the matter has to be resolved by
a card game between Uncle Buck and the next-door planter
to decide whether the latter will buy Tomey's Turl, or the
former, Tennie. Tomey's Turl turns up to deal.

The congeniality of McCaslin slavery thus contributes
to the central *Go Down Moses* argument, that whites and
blacks comprise a single family within which they have different because complementary roles such as those harm-
lessly demonstrated by Tomey's Turl's ritualistic escapes.
Within the secure structure of the plantation, moreover, it
may not be necessary to maintain these roles absolutely.
The masters are generous, the slaves retain their pride. The
runaway Tomey's Turl never deigns to actually run. When
the pursuing McCaslins catch sight of him riding a mule
ahead of them on the trail (he always escapes on a mule)
they spur forward to catch him; "being a nigger, Tomey's
Turl should have jumped down and run for it afoot as soon
as he saw them. But he didn't; maybe Tomey's Turl had
been running off from Uncle Buck for so long that he had
even got used to running away like a white man would do
it" (p. 13). So he remains soberly mounted while still man-
aging to ford the river before the others reach it. Even the
wolfhounds know that the chase is *pro-forma:* reaching the
runaway they desert outright to become yapping puppies
asking only to be scratched.

"Was" thus opens *Go Down Moses* in an apologetic
vein which reaches its nadir in the title story closing the
collection. Here instead of a McCaslin it is Gavin Stevens,
whose presence always bodes conservatism, who is the
central white man. Samuel Beauchamp, the grandson and
last descendant of Lucas (who, along with the McCaslins,

bows out before *Go Down Moses* comes to this sorry end) has gone North and become involved with the Chicago underworld. The inevitable has happened and he now awaits execution for killing a policeman. His grandmother Molly wants his body brought home and prevails on Miss Worsham, an aristocratic lady with whom she "grew up together as sisters would," to arrange it. Miss Worsham in turn enlists Stevens' aid in buying an expensive coffin (everyone in town rushes to contribute to its purchase) and giving Samuel a decent burial, even to local newspaper coverage, so that the illiterate Molly may always treasure the clipping.

But the story itself has some difficulty believing in this togetherness. Its confidence seems especially shaken at the end when Faulkner visualizes directly the black community's mourning of Samuel and, as always led truer by his extraordinary imagination than by his intellect, evokes an ominous bitterness even in the grateful Molly. For instance, the title "Go Down Moses" refers with unpleasant irony to the biblical incantations she chants at the wake. " 'Sold my Benjamin,' " Molly keens, " 'Roth Edmonds sold him. . . . Sold him in Egypt' " (p. 285). Of course (as Stevens unavailingly tries to explain to her, and as Faulkner seems to want to believe), Edmonds has had nothing to do with Samuel's fatal career. In fact, the story implies clearly that Samuel would have done far better to stay home, among the McCaslins, the Edmonds, and the Stevenses. It is the North and the modern world breaking down the old structures that Stevens and, on that level, Faulkner too, consider responsible for her grandson's fall. On this side of the argument the story describes how in Chicago Samuel discarded his Southern identity along with the old virtues of hard work and honesty. The opening portrait of the transformed Samuel makes the point vividly.

The negroid hair had been treated. . . . He wore one of those sports costumes called ensembles in the men's shop advertisements, . . . and they had cost too much and were draped too much, with too many pleats; and he half lay on the steel cot in the steel cubicle . . . smoking cigarettes and answering in a voice which was anything under the sun but a southern voice or even a negro voice. . . . (p. 277)

Who can Molly blame if he became a murderer too? Samuel here only recalls Simon's son Caspey, who, returning from the First World War, rebelled against his father's traditional humility and demanded immediate equality. Neither Caspey nor Samuel are ready for it, as Faulkner explained elsewhere,[10] and they would only abuse it—and yet they

---

[10] A letter from Faulkner to his former butler, Paul E. Pollard, *New York Times,* August 3, 1967. Paul E. Pollard worked for Faulkner as a butler in 1956–57. He subsequently wrote to Faulkner asking for a contribution to the National Association for the Advancement of Colored People, of which Mr. Pollard was a local officer. This was Faulkner's reply:

Charlottesville Va.
24 February 1960

Dear Pollard:

Mrs. Faulkner and I were glad to hear from you and Elizabeth, as we always are, and hope to resume our old friendship here in Charlottesville someday.

I cannot send you this money. I will try to explain why. In the past I contributed indirectly to your organization since I believed it was the only organization which offered your people any hope. But recently it has seemed to me that the organization is making mistakes. Whether it instigates them, or merely condones and takes advantage of them, it is anyway on the side of, in favor of, actions which will do your people harm, by building up to a situation where the white people who hate and grieve over the injustice which your people have to suffer, will be forced to choose either for or against their own people, and they too, the ones

are not so easily dismissed for the author very uncharacteristically steps out front to deliver his verdict: Samuel's ideas are bad because he is bad and he is bad because he was born so, with "something in him from the father who begot and deserted him and who was now in the State Penitentiary for manslaughter—some seed not only violent but dangerous and bad." Nothing there to reflect on anyone. The matter should be settled, but Molly's accusation of the white South is so powerful (so telling?) that it frightens

---

which your people consider the best among my people, will have to choose the side of the rest of the white people.

I agree with your own two great men: Booker T. Washington and Dr. Carver. Any social justice and equality which is compelled to your people by nothing but law and police force, will vanish as soon as the police force is removed, unless the individual members of your race have earned the right to it. As I see it, your people must earn by being individually responsible to bear it, the freedom and equality they want and should have. As Dr. Carver said, "We must make the white people need us, want us to be in equality with them."

I think that your organization is not doing that. Years ago, I set aside a fund of money which I am using, and will continue to use, in education, to teach the people of your race to earn the right to equality, and to show the white people that they are and will be responsible to keep it.

In Dr. Carver's words, make, compel, the white people to want them equal, not just to accept them in equality because police or military bayonets compel them to, and that only until the bayonets are removed again.

As I see it, if the people of your race are to have equality and justice as human beings in our culture, the majority of them have got to be changed completely from the way they now act. Since they are a minority, they must behave better than white people. They must be more responsible, more honorable, more moral, more industrious, more literate and educated. They, not the law, have got to compel the white people to say, Please come out and be equal with us. If the individual Negro does not do this by getting himself educated and trained in responsibility and morality, there will be more and more trouble in individual cases.

That is what I am using my money for, in individual cases.
Sincerely your friend,
William Faulkner

even unflappable Gavin. He attends the wake and it is on this occasion that he argues with Molly that Edmonds is not responsible. But no one there listens and Stevens suddenly panics. "He rose quickly. Miss Worsham rose too, but he did not wait for her to precede him. He went down the hall fast, almost running; he did not even know whether she was following him or not. *Soon I will be outside,* he thought. *Then there will be air, space, breath.*" And all the way he can hear the voices:

> 'Sold him in Egypt and now he dead.'
> 'Oh yes, Lord. Sold him in Egypt.'
> 'Sold him in Egypt.'
> 'And now he dead.'
> 'Sold him to Pharaoh.'
> 'And now he dead.' (p. 286)

This was not the text blacks chanted from twenty years earlier in *The Sound and the Fury.* Mammy Dilsey had brought her white children to church with her and committed herself to everlasting patience and humility. She gave thanks for the freedom she would have in the next world; she celebrated the white man's savior who had " 'died dat dem whut sees en believes shall never die. Breddren, O breddren, I sees de doom crack en hears de golden horns shoutin down de glory en de arisen dead whut got de blood en de ricklickshun of de Lamb!' " [11]

"Go Down Moses" would be, therefore, one of the most conservative pieces in the book, but the wake the story describes also demonstrates Faulkner's sensitivity to a new

[11] *The Sound and the Fury,* p. 208.

tenor in black attitudes, even though he did not sympa-
thize with it intellectually. That sensitivity is enormously
impressive and scenes like this one undoubtedly dramatize
his genius as a writer while they also reveal the limitations
of what Irving Howe has termed abstractly Faulkner's "intellect" and what I would rather call his ideology. For although he seems to realize that the old racial ways can no
longer work, he is unwilling to abandon them or even to
reconsider the racist assumptions which they enacted. By
the end of Go Down Moses, the McCaslin-Edmonds-
Beauchamp family has disintegrated, and not only in the
plot of the book but in Faulkner's imagination as well. The
McCaslin construct implying the existence of a single
Southern "family" cannot survive in the atmosphere of that
hostile wake. But since Faulkner yet retained the construct's racial assumptions, the alternative he created to it
embodied them as well. When Stevens and his nephew
come to the fore in Intruder in the Dust, they also find
ways to preserve the old hierarchy, though not in the Mc-
Caslin-Edmonds guise of family relations.

The search in Go Down Moses for a more viable
modus vivendi with blacks is intrinsically a formal search
for a literary way to depict blacks somewhat differently
than they appeared traditionally in white Southern writing.
The ambiguities and outright contradictions of Lucas Beauchamp as a character dramatize Faulkner's reluctance to do
much more than dress him up. (Appropriately, one of his
most frequently mentioned traits is a hat inherited from
McCaslin, and a gold watch-chain similarly acquired, which
he wears ostentatiously draped across his vest whenever he
feels the need for extra presence.) The central literary issue

in Faulkner's treatment of Lucas, however, is not how he looks but how he sounds, and he sounds much worse than he looks. Except in the course of his struggle with Edmonds over Molly in "The Fire and the Hearth" (and then in the dubious guise of his pride at being a McCaslin) Faulkner never directly dramatizes Lucas' own consciousness of being equal to whites. There are of course numerous instances of one or another Edmonds and of Ike McCaslin thinking that Lucas is their peer, that his blood is equal to, or even better than, theirs, and his spirit more stalwart (this especially from Ike who fears Lucas' contempt for his renunciation). But these testimonials fail somehow to persuade; indeed in some cases they rebound to the favor of the white man, whose humility and tolerance they demonstrate. On the contrary, when we do enter Lucas' mind, as in the first section of "The Fire and the Hearth," we witness only the foolishness about the whiskey still or his silly dream of buried gold. And when Lucas speaks directly he sounds no different, only perhaps more impudent, than the stereotype of a very shrewd but ultimately child-like darky.

In all the stories which concern Lucas the narration occurs on two levels. One recounts actual events and Lucas' cleverness in getting them to go his way. The other hovers overhead to remind us, incongruously, that this busy little man (only once and through the eyes of Zack Edmonds, is he described as moving with dignified deliberation) is entitled to our respect, even to our admiration. But if he is, why are we and the white McCaslins talking over his head? The problem of narrative voice is a familiar one but especially important here where ostensibly the black character is no longer an object of fear or ridicule, but an equal of (however different and separate from) the author, and such as the McCaslins, the Compsons, and the Stevenses.

It is interesting to note that the fact that among the blacks of *Go Down Moses* even Lucas is finally lacking an equal voice affects not only his own credibility but that of the whites as well. This is especially evident in Ike McCaslin, who seems at times curiously out of focus. Faulkner seems not quite certain whether Ike's refusal of the McCaslin plantation constitutes renunciation or surrender. On one level this ambivalence is the same as that manifested in the treatment of Bayard's inability to carry on after his brother's death in *Sartoris,* and of Quentin's suicide in *The Sound and the Fury.* But in *Absalom, Absalom!* Faulkner had concluded with despair that the past really could not be overcome, and that for the class Quentin Compson represents, the Götterdammerung was at hand. Although it purchases some time yet, Ike's conception that the purpose of a continued white hegemony is to work out the white curse implies essentially the same view. If it is not so convincing here as it was earlier, the reason lies in the lesser presence of past blacks than whites. The tragedy of Thomas Sutpen is simply much more compelling than any Ike uncovers in his own ancestry.

Another way of putting it is that, unlike Quentin and Bayard, Ike cannot identify with the figures of the past he recalls. So when the focus of the investigation in the recalling plot shifts from the masters to the slaves, instead of becoming the more vivid for being morally clearer, the vision blurs. Ike's soul-searching seems overly subjective, the expression perhaps of a nervous sensibility rather than, as was Quentin's, sensitivity to external causes. Yet the past that Ike explores is neither abstract nor subjective: he reads it in the actual records of the McCaslin plantation, "that chronicle which was a whole land in miniature, which multiplied and compounded was the entire South" (p. 224). This is much more concrete, more "real" than any evidence offered in the prior recalling plots but what it lacks is the personal validation of an independent black voice.

On balance then, in the ethical framework of Yoknapatawpha, Ike's class suicide seems uncalled for. Faulkner obviously finds much more attractive the responsible stance of Charles Mallison, the young nephew of Gavin Stevens, who proves that there is nothing irrevocable about the way whites have treated blacks. He will do better, not in repudiation of his fellows but out of a "fierce desire that they should be perfect,"

because they were his and he was theirs, that furious intolerance of any one single jot or tittle less than absolute perfection—that furious almost instinctive leap and spring to defend them from anyone anywhere so that he might excoriate them himself without mercy since they were his own and he wanted no more save to stand with them unalterable and impregnable: one shame if shame must be, one expiation since expiation must surely be but above all one unalterable.[12]

It is for sentiments like these that *Intruder in the Dust* was dubbed Faulkner's answer to the Civil Rights Movement. Gavin Stevens sums it all up in a barely fictionalized speech promising that the South will set "Sambo" free, though "it won't be next Tuesday." (One recalls Ike's "someday"

[12] William Faulkner, *Intruder in the Dust* (New York, 1948), pp. 209–10.

which was one or two thousand years away.) But, Stevens warns, if the federal government insists on immediate integration, it will find Southerners united to defend their way of life which is rooted in "homogeneity" that everywhere else "the coastal spew of Europe" has destroyed (p. 155).

But this comes later. At the beginning of the novel Faulkner picks up the thread of his development of an equal-but-separate black by reintroducing Lucas Beauchamp. Molly, his Mammy wife, who ended *Go Down Moses* so unfortunately, has died and Lucas lives "solitary, kinless and intractable, apparently not only without friends even in his own race but proud of it (p. 23)." Faulkner, who elsewhere recommended that blacks "cease forevermore thinking like a Negro and acting like a Negro," [13] looks with favor on this isolation which represents Lucas' refusal to be a nigger. But lower-class white Yoknapatawphans are not so ready to welcome Lucas out of the depths. "Every white man in that whole section of the country had been thinking about him for years: *We got to make* him a nigger. . . . He's got to admit he's a nigger (p. 40)." In this they are neither arbitrary nor sadistic, but motivated by an unexamined impulse to preserve their orderly universe. And so when Lucas is found standing over the corpse of a white man shot by Lucas' own gun, everyone assumes with relief that at last Lucas has "admitted his blackness." (He is, of course, innocent.) Gavin Stevens explains to his nephew how an ordinary decent man like the local storekeeper can come to participate in lynching a black whom he considers has stepped out of line.

[13] William Faulkner, *Essays, Speeches and Public Letters,* edited by James B. Meriwether, N.Y., 1966, p. 157.

He has nothing against what he calls niggers. If you ask him, he will probably tell you he likes them even better than some white folks he knows and he will believe it. They are probably constantly beating him out of a few cents here and there in his store and probably even picking up things. . . . All he requires is that they act like niggers. Which is exactly what Lucas is doing: blew his top and murdered a white man . . . and now the white people will take him out and burn him, all regular and in order and themselves acting exactly as he is convinced Lucas would wish them to act: like white folks; both of them observing implicitly the rules: the nigger acting like a nigger and the white folks acting like white folks and no real hard feeling on either side . . . once the fury is over. (pp. 48–49)

Intruder in the Dust is altogether opposed to this attitude of course. But it is finally a limited opposition taking on only mechanical black and white stereotypes while validating the enlightened prejudices of Stevens, who like Faulkner was willing to accept integration once blacks became worthy of it.[14]

Just at first, though, the fictional situation seems ambiguous, offering not only to prove the uniqueness of Lucas, but perhaps to disprove all stereotypes. When he learns that Lucas has been arrested for murder and that all Jefferson is rather glad of the opportunity to enforce his nigger status, Charles Mallison is reminded of a difficult encounter he himself had with Lucas four years earlier. Then only a boy, he one day slipped and fell into an icy stream. Beauchamp happened by and took the bedraggled child to his own home. Later, dry and fed, Charles drew himself up to his full stature as a young nobleman and of-

[14] *Essays, Speeches and Public Letters*, pp. 157–58.

fered to pay this man he considered something like a serf.
Lucas, however, professed not to understand what the
money was for, and thus effectively made the white boy a
guest in his black home, a traumatic event that shook
Charles to the core of his racist assumptions. Before, he
had simply accepted the "warm reek" of a quilt Lucas
handed him as "that unmistakable odor of Negroes," but
afterwards he wonders whether perhaps

that smell were really not the odor of a race nor even actually of poverty but perhaps of a condition: an idea: a belief: an acceptance, a passive acceptance by them themselves of the idea that being Negroes they were not
supposed to have facilities to wash properly or often or
even to bathe often even without the facilities to do it with:
that in fact it was a little to be preferred that they did not.
(p. 11)

Similarly, before Lucas refused payment for it, the "nigger
food"

was exactly what he had expected, it was what Negroes ate,
obviously because it was what they liked, what they chose;
not . . . that out of their long chronicle this was all
they had had a chance to learn to like except the ones who
ate out of white folks' kitchens, but that they had elected
this out of all eating because this was their palates and their
metabolism. (p. 13)

The interest in these explanations lies, of course, not in
their content, but in Charles's attempt itself to explain envi-
ronmentally and culturally qualities and traits he had hith-
erto considered innate. Perhaps the most telling image expressing this new possibility for Faulkner's black characters
is a photograph he sees of Molly which at first he doesn't

recognize because it was taken without the "headrag." "And that was it, she had hair." With this symbolic removal of Mammy's headpiece, Mallison realizes that Lucas is a man "inside a Negro's skin but that was all" (pp. 14, 6–7, 18).

But it isn't all, for Lucas' shortcomings as an emancipated black man have been carried over from *Go Down Moses*. His scornful defiance of redneck threats when he is first arrested takes the familiar form of pride in his white ancestry. " 'I'm a McCaslin,' " he tells a red-faced rustic whom he despises for not even being an Edmonds. And the same contrast as in the earlier work between what we are told of Lucas and what he says for himself undermines even the triumphant image of Molly without her kerchief. For, as explained by Lucas, the photograph in fact endorses the stereotype it otherwise challenges in Charles's understanding. Lucas had insisted that Molly remove her headrag because " 'I didn't want no field nigger picture in the house.' " (p. 5).

Actually neither Lucas nor any lower-class white but only Charles questions the old ways in *Intruder in the Dust*. This is in accord with Faulkner's plea to the South to accept integration in the name of its Confederate heritage:

Our ancestors were not afraid like this—our grandfathers who fought at First and Second Manassas . . . let alone those who survived that and had the additional and even greater courage and endurance to resist and survive Reconstruction and so preserved to us something of our present heritage. Why are we, descendants of that blood and inheritors of that courage, afraid? . . . What has happened to us in only a hundred years? [15]

[15] *Essays, Speeches and Public Letters*, p. 101.

By the same logic, Charles claims that in championing Lucas he only carries on the proud traditions which the South upheld in the Civil War. However contradictory this may seem, it defines exactly the characteristic Faulknerian genre of the critical apologia which all of his black writing represents.

One of the important aspects of this genre in *Go Down Moses* was the discord it generated between the book's rhetoric and its dramatizations, in short, between what it said and what it did. This happens in *Intruder in the Dust* as well, where there is an even sharper contrast between Lucas' vaunted independence and his actual role in the plot. After the first chapter, Lucas is confined to jail and thus effectively out of action. It is now up to Mallison (and the aristocratic Miss Habersham)[16] to prove him innocent. It is true that Lucas tells them where to find the evidence they need, but this hardly offsets his enforced passivity; he can only await deliverance, locked once more into the dependence he had briefly escaped in the first chapter (although even there only partially since we saw him not directly but through the medium of Charles's memory). The real hero of *Intruder in the Dust* is, of course, Charles Mallison, who combines Ike McCaslin's integrity with the responsibility and confidence Bayard Sartoris displayed in *The Unvanquished*. The last of Faulkner's young men to confront their heritage, he is also the most conservative, a Tory who never doubts the right of his class to rule. He accepts without question his Uncle Gavin's political sociology of Yoknapatawpha. There is a fine eighteenth-century ra-

[16] Miss Habersham is, like Miss Worsham in *Go Down Moses*, a spinster lady of aristocratic lineage who feels obligated to the descendants of her parents' and grandparents' slaves.

tionality to the world Stevens diagrams for his nephew, a world peacefully apportioned according to everyone's preference and capability. It takes all kinds, he tells Charles; in the South there are three basic groups:

people who chose by preference to live [in the hills] on little patches which wouldn't make eight bushels of corn or fifty pounds of lint cotton an acre even if they were not too steep for a mule to pull a plow across (but then they don't want to make the cotton anyway, only the corn and not too much of that because it really doesn't take a great deal of corn to run a still as big as one man and his sons want to fool with) are people named Gowrie and McCallum and Fraser and Ingum. . . . And in the valleys along the rivers, the broad rich easy land where a man can raise something he can sell openly in daylight, the people named Littlejohn and Greenleaf and Armstead and Millingham and Bookwright. . . . And the ones named Sambo, they live in both, they elect both because they can stand either because they can stand anything. (pp. 148–49)

The fact that without him Lucas would probably have been lynched for a murder he did not commit does not seriously challenge Mallison's belief in the fundamental justice of this society. After all, it was his ancestors who "evoluted him" and through him they now vindicate themselves. The relationship between Stevens and Mallison dramatizes this process. At first Stevens thinks that Lucas is guilty and refuses to help his nephew investigate further. When Charles and Miss Habersham bring him contrary evidence, however, Stevens readily concedes they are right and in fact takes a certain paternal pride in Mallison's deeper perception. Indeed all Yoknapatawpha's better whites are eager to do the right thing. It is the local constable who saves Lucas from the lower-class mob who would have executed him on the spot, the sheriff and his deputy who finally transfer him from the prison to the deputy's own home to keep him safe, and Gavin Stevens who organizes all these measures to ensure Lucas a fair trial. They have all believed him guilty but are happy to acknowledge Charles's evidence and aid him in his investigation (which ultimately leads to the dead man's brother, who is most assuredly not one of them). Indeed the real threat to Lucas comes from Beat Four, a ghetto of "brawlers and farmers and fox-hunters . . . and whiskey-makers" where even "peace-officers from town" are not safe (pp. 35–36). All this recalls the strikingly parallel situation of *Light in August*, except that here the respectable white men do their duty triumphantly.

Early in *The Sound and the Fury*, Quentin Compson, on his way home from Cambridge, looked out the train window and realized that he had arrived: "there was a nigger on a mule. How long he had been there I didn't know, but he sat straddle of the mule, his head wrapped in a piece of blanket, as if they had been built there with the fence and the road, or with the hill, carved out of the hill itself, like a sign put there saying you are home again." [17]

Near the end of *Intruder in the Dust*, Charles Mallison, speeding to set Lucas Beauchamp free, sees through the car window (the passage has been cited at the beginning of this essay) "the land's living symbol," "a formal group of ritual almost mystic significance the beast the plow and the [black] man integrated in one, foundationed into the frozen wave of their furrow tremendous with effort yet at the same time vacant of progress, ponderable immovable and

[17] *The Sound and the Fury*, p. 72.

immobile like groups of wrestling statuary set against the land's immensity" (p. 147). The images are fundamentally the same, especially in their objectification of the black man whom we see, like the hill and the plow, invested with meaning only through the agency of a white observer. And the constancy of Faulkner's race assumptions actually held much longer than this twenty-year span. From Othello, the servile train porter in *Soldiers' Pay* (1926), to *The Reivers* (1962) whose Uncle Ned titters "hee hee hee" and gets into mischief directly "Boss" turns his back, Faulkner's black characters did, in fact, endure.

5

A Comedy of Rustics

Toward the end of his career Faulkner wrote three novels which center on characters of "redneck," lower-class white origin. Ironically, however, the thematic structure of these works, constituting the Snopes trilogy of *The Hamlet* (1940), *The Town* (1957), and *The Mansion* (1959), suggests that the author had finally settled at the conservative pole of his ideological ambivalence. Overall the novels depict a futile battle waged by Yoknapatawpha agrarians ostensibly against the commercialization of their county. Gavin Stevens, who leads the forces of light, is the scion of one of the county's first and most distinguished families, with extensive holdings in men and land long before the Civil War. That he personally has nothing to do with agriculture enables Gavin to embody the abstract qualities which Faulkner admired in the aristocracy without visibly sharing its fatal responsibility for slavery and the misuse of the land. In Stevens, Faulkner can ignore the socioeconomic issues at the heart of *Absalom, Absalom!* The result is abstract but untrammeled conservatism, with Stevens recalling the sounder aspects of the mythical cavalier. He is a gentleman and a scholar (Harvard and Heidelberg universities) and, as district attorney, a responsible statesman as well. Allied with him in his struggle to preserve the traditional order is V. K. Ratliff, who, like other folk philosophers in Southern literature,[1] expounds a Tory common sense, and Will Varner, who, for all his sturdy homeliness, is lord of countless serfs. They are assisted by Gavin's young nephew Charles Mallison, who figures prominently in *Intruder in the Dust,* there as here representing the youthful hope of the South. The enemy are the mercenary Snopeses, rednecks, croppers, poor-whites, white trash: the traditional Southern villains. It would seem, then, that Faulkner had definitively come over to the planter's side, and much of the trilogy so indicates. But overall and in the end, the Snopes saga represents not a conservative resolution of the conflict I have been tracing but its last crisis. And here again the author's ideological difficulties have formal repercussions. There is a significant decline in artistic quality from *The Hamlet* to *The Town,* with only a partial recovery in the last of the three novels, *The Mansion.*

Although Gavin Stevens holds the position of honor among the defenders of Yoknapatawpha County, Will Varner is more directly embattled: his daughter and part of his land will constitute Flem Snopes's first important win.

---

[1] I am referring to such homespun worthies as Charles H. Smith's Bill Arp, who, in *The Farm and the Fireside* (Atlanta, 1892), averred he so loved his landlord that he would "about as leave belong to him as to be free," and the good Tom Nettles in William Gilmore Simms's *As Good As Comedy* (Philadelphia, 1852).

(Appropriately it is Jody Varner, the son of Will, who sights the first Snopes in the county.) Varner is an interesting figure, the type of the planter in homespun who had already appeared in *Westward Ho!*, for example, or wherever a writer was uneasy about the aristocratic airs of the cavalier. In Faulkner's own time, Hodding Carter defined this homely type as, "primarily," he explained, "simple farmers on a large scale." [2] Faulkner liked to make the same distinction between "my country," which was "frontier," and "the common picture of the South" as "all magnolias and crinoline and Grecian portals . . . which was true only around the fringes of the South. Not in the interior, the backwood." [3] On the surface this would seem fairly accurate. But the real message in Carter's rustic characterization emerges when he concludes that "not even the most painstaking demolition" (his own presumably one) "of the river planter myth" "can successfully dispute that as a class they were also amazingly hospitable and tenacious and clannishly loyal and generous; good livers who admired and sought to own beautiful homes, fast horses, and not infrequently a comely slave woman or two." Mindful of their democratic image, he terms these aspirations "earthy longings, but not without merit." [4] The outcome of this "demolition" is clear: the old myth rises strong in all its essential aspects and is, moreover, vindicated by the borrowed virtues of the "simple farmer."

Faulkner had earlier achieved the same effect in his depiction of the McCaslins, slaveowners who rather resemble Sir Walter Scott's peasants than his noblemen. One of their neighbors, "Mr. Hubert," has a sister named Sophon-

[2] Hodding Carter, *Lower Mississippi* (New York, 1942), p. 205.
[3] *Faulkner in the University*, p. 131.   [4] Carter, p. 205.

siba, who wants her brother and his rough friends to be more cultured. She herself wears a ribbon at her throat, carries a trained bird on her wrist, and calls the muddy plantation, "Warwick," "after the place in England that she said Mr. Hubert was probably the true Earl of." [5] Her absurd pretensions cause the others to appear democratic by contrast, while the actual character of the plantation economy remains unexamined. Gruff and rather coarse, Will Varner descends from this typology. He enables Faulkner to so blur the controversial character of the aristocrat as to embody in Varner the whole of the agrarian cause, apparently forgetting that Flem too has a rural identity. This is only temporary, for later, in *The Mansion*, a Snopes will reclaim his agrarian character and for a time generate a situation in which class lines emerge much as they do in *Absalom, Absalom!* But the initial and central structure of the Snopes trilogy opposes an agrarian Will Varner (signifying, besides a sturdy rusticity, the Old South, even, by association, the refined ethics and esthetics of Gavin Stevens, his nephew's moderate racial attitudes, and Ratliff's folk wisdom) to petit-merchant Snopes.

But nothing can prevail against the pollution gradually darkening the County skies. In *The Hamlet* Flem conquers the village of Frenchman's Bend by acquiring control of various Varner enterprises and marrying Eula Varner, the local incarnation of a combined Venus and Ceres. (Flem himself is, of course, both impotent and sterile.) The invasion creeps on to the county seat, Jefferson, where Snopes ascends to the presidency of the pointedly named Sartoris Bank. By the end of *The Town*, Flem has won the

[5] William Faulkner, "Was," *Go Down Moses,* p. 11.

field. *The Mansion* records his fall when he is assassinated by a poor relation whose old-fashioned trust in tribal loyalty Flem has betrayed for the sake of his own advance into the modern world.

The Snopeses are humorous folk, which many have taken to prove that Faulkner had a lighter side—except that much of the humor is darkly serious. The genre is traditional to the South and depends upon certain political assumptions concerning the social character of its clowns. Southern humorists, dating back to their establishment as a literary school with Augustus Longstreet's *Georgia Scenes,* had long ago described villainous rednecks whose amorality and lack of culture provoked horrified amusement among their superiors. But, as Kenneth Lynn argues persuasively in *Mark Twain and Southwestern Humor,* the comic treatment of Southern poor whites disguised serious warnings of a redneck threat to the established order. Most of those writing in the genre were Whigs. Johnson J. Hooper, the "journalist of secession" and famed author of *The Adventures of Simon Suggs,* was one such. His Simon Suggs, a caricature of Andrew Jackson, is the devil in a hell of popular anarchy.[6] The message of Southwestern humor long retained its clarity. As late as 1964 *The Mississippi Quarterly* was praising the humorists as moral men "naturally . . . scornful of squatters who were willing to use the land as long as they did not have to pay for it and to accept responsibility as citizens." [7]

[6] Johnson J. Hooper, *The Adventures of Simon Suggs* (Americus, Ga., 1928).

[7] "Scholarship in Southwestern Humor—Past and Present," *The Mississippi Quarterly,* xvii (Spring 1964). In the same issue John K. Betterworth, "The Humor of the Old Southwest: Yesterday and Today," ex-

The political assumptions of the humorists, therefore, were not essentially different from those underlying plantation fiction. Indeed, sometimes the same man wrote in both genres, as did the author of "The Great Bear of Arkansas," who also answered *Uncle Tom's Cabin* in *The Master's House.* Cultural historians who thought they were reading the other side of the Southern story in the work of the humorists, who found in it a way at last to raise "the veil of smug respectability for a refreshing view of the real thing," [8] were therefore largely misled by formal differences. For Ransy Sniffle (a rustic of Longstreet's) is really "a projection in outrageous caricature of a political conservative's exacerbation." [9] In contrast, through the wise narrator whose commentary typically framed the action of the tale, the humorists projected precisely the plantation myth's image of a cultured aristocrat who was obviously meant to rule the South.

One Southern writer, wondering why the Confederate flag "once the battle ensign of brave men . . . [has] come to stand for raw racism and hoodlum defiance of the law" quite accurately located the Snopeses in the ideological universe of the humorist tradition. Walker Percy has explained the "spectacular" change in the South as resulting from the defeat of "the old moderate tradition of the planter-lawyer-statesman class" and "the consequent collapse of the alliance between the 'good' white man and the

---

presses the fear that humor is being "nationalized" out of existence. It is already considered poor taste to make race jokes, he notes, and soon the welfare state will outlaw class humor as well.

[8] W. Stanley Hoole, *Alias Simon Suggs* (Montgomery, Ala., 1952), pp. 29–30.

[9] Kenneth Lynn, *Mark Twain and Southwestern Humor* (Boston, 1959), p. 72.

Negro. . . . To use Faulkner's personae," he wrote succinctly, "the Gavin Stevenses have disappeared and the
Snopeses have won." [10] The dire prophecies of Hooper
and Harris have been realized; Longstreet would have con-
curred, shuddering. The Whig Götterdammerung has come
and in its wake the "uncouth, unclean, [and] lawless" poor
whites have successfully taken over the ruined South.

Like Simon Suggs, therefore, Flem Snopes is a petty
opportunist worming his way to repulsive gains through a
decaying social structure. But in reality, of course, big
businessmen with redneck origins were rather exceptional
in Faulkner's time. Men like Will Varner, planters who also
became merchants "so that they could have more control
over their tenants," [11] constituted then the greatest
number of store owners and commercial entrepreneurs,
while the really large corporations like those which own
most of the land in the Missississippi Delta were frequently
controlled by Northern or foreign interests. When the National Emergency Council reported in 1938 (approximately
the time when Faulkner was writing the final version of *The
Hamlet*) that a key factor in Southern "underdevelopment"
was the role of extra-regional capital, it was recognizing a
situation which had prevailed since the nineteenth century.[12] Only two years prior to the Report, Governor Hugh
White of Mississippi began implementing a "Balance Agriculture with Industry Plan" (BAWI), which was "based
upon an appeal to Northern industry to run away from

[10] Walker Percy, "Mississippi: The Fallen Paradise," *The South Today,*
Harper's Special Supplement (April 1965).

[11] Jacqueline P. Bull, "The General Merchant in the Economic History
of the New South," *The Journal of Southern History,* xviii (February 1952).

[12] As C. Vann Woodward establishes in *Origins of the New South,*
1877–1913.

troublesome Northern unions to the promised docility of low-wage Southern labor." [13]

Moreover, after the land boom in 1875 in which the North and England were the chief participants,[14] there was never a clear distinction between landowners and capitalists. C. Vann Woodward has described a capitalistic monopoly of land, much of it based on Northern money, which developed in the post-Reconstruction South. Large corporate plantations, like the Duke Tobacco Company in North Carolina, which also owned the Duke Power Company,[15] tended to control all the important sectors of state industry. The threat to the traditional socioeconomic structure of the South after the Civil War and in Faulkner's time hardly came from small-time opportunists like Flem Snopes. (Faulkner's indifference to drawing a representative picture of Southern conditions appears also in his description of the Jefferson power plant, which is municipally owned and operated, not a common situation anywhere.) Far from infiltrating their state's economic power centers, rednecks on the farm and off moved about the Southern economy horizontally. Mill towns replaced tenant villages but which were preferable is still a matter of debate. There is, therefore, little historical justification for Flem's steady rise to become eventually "a prominent banker and financier . . . [with] no auspices . . . : fraternal, civic nor military: only finance; not an economy—cotton or cattle or anything else which Yoknapatawpha

---

[13] Jonathan Daniels, "The Ever-Ever Land," *The South Today* (April 1965).

[14] Woodward, *Origins of the New South*, p. 115.

[15] Arthur F. Raper and Ira De A. Reid, *Sharecroppers All* (Chapel Hill, N.C., 1941), p. 195.

County and Mississippi were established on and kept running by, but belonging simply to Money." [16]

What all this means is that by embodying in a redneck the modern threat to the traditional South, Faulkner was not describing something he saw about him, but seeing something he had heard and read previously described. He was accepting the old Whig charge that the great danger to Southern temperance and order lay in the predatory activity of its lowest (white) class. It is an ambiguous acceptance, for Flem becomes a threat only after he discards his agrarian poor-white identity, and his kinfolk back on the farm suffer from his predatoriness right along with everyone else. And of course it is Mink Snopes who finally destroys Flem and thereby presumably Snopesism. Yet the basic social hierarchy of the trilogy reflects acceptance of the old myth.

Thus Faulkner was becoming more conventional and in his way of writing as well, which increasingly recalled Southern literary tradition—not so much the plantation literature, but the complementary body of Southern and Southwestern humor. Of course he was not always firmly convinced of the conservative point of view expressed by this genre, but its earlier practitioners hadn't been either. A certain ambiguity in the narrative viewpoint of Hooper, for example, probably reflects ambiguity in the author's attitude toward his character, a tension between his aristocratic allegiance and the peculiar attraction of the villainous Simon. Although Hooper was staunchly hostile to Suggsism, he came at times perilously close to glorying in Suggs's successes. One senses a perverse pleasure on his

[16] William Faulkner, *The Mansion* (New York, 1959), p. 419.

part when Simon takes particulary vicious advantage of his victims, a feeling originating perhaps partly from misanthropic disillusionment, but also in part a response to vernacular vitality. The author of *Sut Lovingood* was even more alienated by the weakness of the Southern upper class, almost to the point of bitterly identifying with Sut.

Henri Bergson's definition of comedy ("the attitudes, gestures and movements of the human body are laughable in exact proportion as that body reminds us of a mere machine") will help to show the pattern of this development. Longstreet's clown in "The Fight" is a grunting object whose comic appeal depends upon our sense of distance. But Harris introduces elements into Sut Lovingood which have the opposite effect of drawing us to his side—we are aware at times that the absurdly violent world in which he lives can cause him pain. Chased by a rampaging bull, he jerks about like a grotesque doll, but he also bleeds. Thus humor is laced with pathos and shades from the Keystone Cops to Charlie Chaplin. Harris handled the too sobering effects of such pathos by isolating it and dividing his characters. While we come increasingly to identify with Sut, his victims, such as a grotesquely Fat Boy who can be fiendishly tortured without feeling the pinch, remain the old-fashioned clowns. But this was at best an uneasy compromise.[17]

When Faulkner depicts the Snopeses as allegorical abstractions he reaps the same benefits as Longstreet in being able to ignore his characters' inner humanity. Such treat-

[17] The development of the "vernacular voice" which represents this process has been discussed by Henry Nash Smith, *Mark Twain, The Development of a Writer* (Cambridge, Mass., 1962), and Kenneth Lynn, *Mark Twain and Southwestern Humor.*

ment was useful in circumventing his still unresolved ambiguity about Southern society. The pattern, "Flem the evil redneck" versus Gavin "the moral aristocrat," was both unreal and contradictory to Faulkner's persistent Jeffersonian impulses. His imagination would more easily accept a battle between Gavin the abstractly traditional Southerner and Flem the absolute villain. But as it had the characters of the humorists, an image of real rednecks shadowed Faulkner's mythical ciphers and, at times, breathed greater depth into them.

"The Spotted Horses" and "Horseswap" episodes of *The Hamlet* each illustrate this process and its thematic implications. "The Spotted Horses" depicts one of Flem's particularly villainous exploits. On returning from a Texas honeymoon, Flem is followed at a suspiciously close interval by a stranger leading a string of wild ponies. The stranger holds an auction (amidst wide speculation as to whether Flem owns the horses) and by various tricks of the trade succeeds in selling all the untamable horses. When their new owners attempt to harness the horses, they stampede, injuring many farmers, and escape into the hills. Since no one knows whether Flem owned the ponies or not and the stranger has vanished, there is no one from whom to demand a refund and the yokels are left with nothing.

This tale represents some important modifications of the genre. As handled by Longstreet, for example, it traditionally consists of a narrator who tells an amusing anecdote about a trickster and his victim, neither of whom ever speaks directly to the reader nor himself sees the humor in the situation. The narrator and the projected reader, however, share a level of perception which enables them to perceive the absurdity of it all and especially entitles them to laugh at it. It is clearly important that this difference in status be maintained or the humor and its message will both be destroyed. Typically, the events described are outrageously violent and bloody but, by the definition of the form, we need, indeed can, feel no concern for the victims, who themselves feel nothing.

But "The Spotted Horses" is rather different. For one thing it has two of everything, two narrators, two tricksters, and two victims. Ratliff is the main narrator, but Faulkner has introduced a second framing device through periodic mention of a Mrs. Littlejohn, who lives within sight of the auction and whose very sensible activities punctuate and indict the farmers' foolishness. From early in the morning when we see her in the distance lugging in wood to start the fire, to when she takes her clean clothes from the line in the evening, we are conscious of her mute commentary on all the nonsense in the foreground. The trickster figure is also doubled since the auctioneer actually perpetrates the fraud, but presumably at Flem's instance. There are two victims as well: the general group of rednecks and one particularly pathetic victim on whom the story focuses to tell us that his name is Armstid and that he has wasted five irreplaceable dollars on one of the horses when his emaciated children lack food and clothing. Finally, the frame structure is itself modified when Ratliff, who as narrator should remain outside the story, enters the plot, and Flem, who belongs inside, remains mutely on the sidelines. In effect, there are two tales in "The Spotted Horses": one is conventional but the second, like an alter ego, comments on the first. In the conventional story the glib stranger sells the assembled fools something they do not want and cannot use at an exorbitant price. But no one really gets hurt in the process, and when the stampeding horses overturn a wagon of yokels, the wreckage is reminiscent of *The Adventures of Simon Suggs*.

The second story takes such trickery seriously by showing it can inflict real pain on its victims. This element of seriousness is introduced early in the story when Ratliff, who throughout seriously compromises the detached and unfeeling stance of the traditional narrator, joins three farmers squatting around waiting for the auction to begin. He warns them against buying the horses, then falls silent.

Ratliff, invisible in the shadow against the wall made a sound, harsh sardonic, not loud. "Ratliff's laughing." "Don't mind me," Ratliff said. The three speakers had not moved. They did not move now, yet there seemed to gather about the three silhouettes something stubborn, convinced and passive, like children who have been chidden. A bird, a shadow, fleet and dark and swift curved across the moonlight, upward into the pear tree and began to sing; a mockingbird.[18]

The darkness, the ominous shadows, and Ratliff's humorless laughter combine to predict more sorrow than comedy. The characterization of the men as children reinforces this feeling by introducing a motif that recurs twice, the first time in the description of a small boy's almost mystical invulnerability to the wild ponies and again when Mrs. Armstid invokes her children by telling how she earned the money her husband has paid for the useless horse by weaving until late at night to buy shoes for her "chaps." Flem's victims, therefore, become associated on this level

[18] William Faulkner, *The Hamlet*, p. 317.

with innocent childhood, and the vague pathos thus introduced into the story comes into focus in Mrs. Armstid, who is pure victim. Faced with her pathetic appeal, the auctioneer, whose traditional role depends on jolly victims like Sut's "Fat Boy," falls apart entirely and returns her five dollars, reversing his role so far as to try to dissuade her husband from pursuing his stampeding horse. The introduction of suffering has here dissolved the traditional tale by denying its constituency of unfeeling clowns.

If the victim has been shown sensible to pain, so the villain now preys in earnest. Flem steps in to take back the money that the converted auctioneer had returned to Mrs. Armstid. Insensitivity and trickery have thus been revealed to mask real suffering and real evil. Like Mrs. Littlejohn, we don't think it's funny. Faulkner has almost succeeded in using the genre to comment on its own assumptions and thus uncover its ideological basis—but not quite, for he does not go so far as to make the victims, the central clowns, completely human. Mrs. Armstid is more moving but hardly more real as a pathetic figure than was the comic caricature she reverses. Without inner life or a voice of her own she remains an object now of pity rather than laughter.

Because the "Spotted Horses" episode counterpoints comic allegory and sentiment without fusing the two in a "real," conscious human being, it remains split on two distinct levels, containing two sets of characters—and indeed coming to two conclusions. At a county hearing into the fraudulent auction, the victims of the overturned wagon try to get reparations and, failing to do so, make a riotously noisy exit. But Mrs. Armstid, who also seeks justice, accepts her defeat in despairing silence. Faulkner stresses the

poignancy of the scene, describing in detail the worn figure standing frail in the courtroom and the gaunt mule on
which she rides back to her crazed husband and hungry
children. The chapter itself in which "The Spotted Horses"
occurs ends twice, as if to stress its duality. It seems at first
to close with the comic exit described above, then goes on
to record Mink's threat against Flem, which has no immediate relation to the story of the wild horses. "Tell that son of
a bitch, . . . ," [19] mutters Mink, and fades off in a fantasy
of the revenge he will wreak for himself and, in context,
perhaps for Mrs. Armstid.

Faulkner's sympathy for his poor-white characters is
here deep enough to evoke their suffering but not quite
complete enough to let them speak for themselves. And as
long as Mrs. Armstid and her kind remain mute, they cannot at their best behavior really transcend sentimentality.
When in an isolated instance Faulkner has a Snopes speak
for himself, the effect nearly shatters the type. This occurs
when Montgomery Ward Snopes agrees to help Flem trick
Mink into trying to escape from prison, so that Mink, who
has threatened Flem's life, will be punished with an additional term. The circumstances are not important; they
matter only in that "Monty" explains them himself and
thereby briefly blooms into a substantial character who,
despite this cynicism, has the twisted integrity to spell out
the cruel intent of his act and to articulate the moral bankruptcy that leads Flem to ask and him to accept such an er-
rand. Of course there is the first-person narration of Mink's
own story to indicate both the potential impact of the form
and what Faulkner could do with it when he chose. But the
story of Mink is one of the agrarian sections of the trilogy

[19] *The Hamlet,* p. 382.

and not so fully subject to the stultifying effect of the general Snopes conception.

For the most part the three novels are conventionally narrated—by Gavin Stevens or his nephew, Charles Mallison, sometimes directly by the author and by Ratliff, the narrator of "The Spotted Horses," whose characterization also reflects Faulkner's uncertainty about the question of class narrative role. In an attenuated vernacular Ratliff endorses a qualified upper-class ethic. He sometimes ridicules the romantic illusions of Stevens but more often he backs up his gentleman friend whom he resembles in being himself somewhat déclassé. Ratliff is the son of a sharecropper but has become a "drummer" of sewing machines. Thus both are at one remove from their origins in the basic agrarian configuration of the region. But Stevens continues to articulate his class's point of view while Ratliff significantly tries to "improve" his speech and make it more grammatical.[20]

The basic situation of another humorous episode, the

[20] Charles Mallison (Chick) resists Ratliff's efforts but the latter realizes that his folk idiom represents a limit on his social mobility.

Ratliff : ". . . if he . . . dragged her—Chick"
[Charles Mallison]: "Drug," I said "You said 'dragged.' "
Ratliff looked at me [Chick] for a while. "For ten years now . . . I been listening . . . trying to learn—teach myself to say words right. And, jest when I call myself about to learn and I begin to feel a little good over it, here you come . . . correcting me back to what I been trying for ten years to forget."
Chick: "I'm sorry," I said. "I didn't mean it that way. It's because I like the way you say it. When you say it, 'taken' sounds a heap more took than just 'took,' just like 'drug' sounds a heap more dragged than just 'dragged.' "
Ratliff : "And not jest you neither," Ratliff said. "Your uncle too: me saying 'dragged' and him saying 'drug' again, until at last he would say, 'In a free country like this, why aint I got as much right to use your *drug* for my *dragged* as you got to use my *dragged* for your *drug?*' " (*The Town*, pp. 260–61.)

"Horseswap," had already appeared in Longstreet's "Horseswap." In the earlier version, Yellow Blossom (". . . perhaps a *leetle*, jist a *leetle* of the best man at a horseswap that ever trod shoe-leather") trades horses with a farmer who admits his own horse is blind. The trade completed, Yellow Blossom hilariously reveals a horrible sore on the back of the horse he has just traded. The farmer's little son, angered by the laughter at his father's expense, cries out revengefully that the horse the boaster has just acquired is not only blind but stone-deaf and will throw anyone who mounts him. The story ends with the deserved discomfiture of the boaster, as the narrator shakes his head tolerantly at the amusing antics of these peasants. The only one he has sympathy for anyway is the horse.[21]

Faulkner's version is more complicated. Ab Snopes, who has always been "a fool about a horse," sets out to buy his wife a milk separator. On the way he becomes embroiled in a complicated series of "swaps" with a genius named Pat Stamper, and finally returns home with neither separator nor money and with his original horse. His wife then grimly loads her only cow onto a truck and drives off, to return a little later without the cow but with a brand new separator which she uses over and over on the one gallon of milk that the boy Ratliff, an observer to all this, has thoughtfully brought from his father's farm. The intent of the story, to show Ab's vulnerable humanity, directly reverses the goal of the Longstreet original. To accomplish this, the narrator has to communicate the full extent of the rustic's suffering, which means that he must be so close to him that he sees the events as the sufferer himself sees

[21] This tale is included in Augustus Longstreet's *Georgia Scenes* (New York, 1957).

them. Faulkner had achieved this in an earlier version by having a little boy narrate the story about his own parents. In adapting it to *The Hamlet,* Faulkner carried this over by making Ratliff a child and stressing his complete sympathy with Ab. But he still retains a narrator instead of having Ab tell the story himself, and because Ratliff's irony and his sympathy do not quite fuse, this episode operates, like "The Spotted Horses," on two levels. Only at the end of the story do the two levels merge in the definitive image of Mrs. Snopes repeatedly running the single gallon of milk through the separator which "sounded strong as ever, like it could make the milk fly, like it didn't give a whoop whether that milk had been separated once or a hundred times. 'There it goes again,' Ab says. 'It looks like she is fixing to get a heap of pleasure and satisfaction outen it.' " That kind of life could indeed sour a man and it is not surprising that Ab is "plumb curdled." [22] This sociological explanation of Snopes behavior clearly diverges from their prevalent rendition as inherently bad. And in fact this story, which anyway appears in the first of the Snopes novels, written long before the other two, had been conceived even earlier, at just the time Faulkner was writing *Absalom, Absalom!* in 1936. The trilogy moves decisively away from "The Horseswap" toward such episodes as "The Waifs," which totally dehumanizes its redneck characters.

This incident in *The Town* describes the arrival in Jefferson of four wild urchins, the offspring of I. O. Snopes and a Mexican Indian woman. After numerous cannibalistic attacks on local inhabitants including their own relatives, the children are shipped back to their parents, each an unkempt package with a tag wired to its clothing noting

[22] *The Hamlet,* pp. 48, 32.

destination. They speak no English and there are few ves-
tiges of a human physiognomy beneath the tangled hair
which covers their faces. Faulkner calls them wolf-cubs;
they are "four things" wrapped in dirty rags. The "littlest
'un" is of indefinite gender. They come and leave by train;
no one knew of them before and they are immediately
forgotten. They represent the complete flattening of the
Snopeses into mere ciphers. Indeed, Ratliff, who has
always maintained that Yoknapatawpha would have to
expel its Snopeses to be rid of Snopesism, sees the depar-
ture of the wolf-children as the "end of an era . . . the last
and final end of Snopes out-and-out unvarnished behavior
in Jefferson." [23] This episode occurs at the end of *The
Town*, where Faulkner deals almost exclusively with the
nonagrarian, commercial South. Flem's take-over of the hy-
droelectric plant and of the bank, as well as the general
shift of power from planters to financiers and merchants,
all of which *The Town* deals with, are the central concerns
of the trilogy. Yet it is precisely in this context that Faulkner's treatment of the Snopeses becomes most abstract
and recalls the humorist tradition not even as Harris, but as
Longstreet before him had defined it.

[23] *The Town*, pp. 366, 370.

6

Equal to Any, Good as Any

There are two aspects of the Snopes conception which limit its literary potential. The first, which we have been considering, is that in its ideological assumptions, "Snopes" vitiated much of the sympathy the author felt for poorer farmers, a sympathy whose tense relationship to his aristocratic biases was one of his most powerful inspirations. This drawback is evident in even the best parts of the Snopes novels, in such relatively successful sections as "The Spotted Horses" and indeed in much of *The Hamlet*. The second problem, also inherent in the area of the Snopeses, is that it simply did not apply to the subjects Faulkner wanted to treat—so that when these subjects, issues relating to the South's commercialization, became the central concern of the works, the Snopeses appear curiously irrelevant and their new stage barren. The latter is probably the main reason that the agrarian sections of the books are the best. They are in fact even written differently. Briefly, the more realistic rural episodes tend to work symbolically while those having to do with town life as well as the overall definition of Snopesism are schematically allegorical. The two styles conflict throughout the trilogy, whose thematic and ideological development can be read in the progress of the conflict. The distinction between them will become clear in application to the text.

In the opening paragraph of *The Hamlet,* the village of Frenchman's Bend is discovered as "a section of rich river-bottom country lying twenty miles southeast of Jefferson." The way Faulkner then informs this specific description with meaning differs significantly from the allegorical genre dominant in the Snopes stories. Frenchman's Bend, he writes, is "hill-cradled and remote, definite yet without boundaries." This last phrase describes beautifully how symbols generally function by enlarging the definition of a specific object or event to involve other levels of meaning. Here the village is first a village with a definite, self-sufficient identity, but it can also embody certain abstract ideas which extend from it. It does so very fruitfully in the ensuing scene. Ratliff, who has been out of town, returns to learn of the impending marriage of Flem Snopes and Eula Varner. Feeling "as though the gods themselves had tunneled all the concentrated bright June onto a dung heap breeding pismires," he approaches Frenchman's Bend:

Now he could see the village proper—the store, the blacksmith shop, the metal roof of the gin with a thin rapid shimmer of exhaust above the stack . . . the dry, dust-laden air vibrated steadily to the rapid beat of the engine, though so close were the steam and the air in temperature that no exhaust was visible but merely a thin feverish shimmer of mirage. The very hot, vivid air, which seemed to be filled with the slow laborious plaint of laden wagons, smelled of lint; wisps of it clung among the soot-stiffened roadside weeds and small bits of cotton lay imprinted by hoof and wheel marks into the trodden dust. He could see the wagons too, waiting to advance . . . onto the scales and then beneath the suction pipe where Jody Varner would now be.[1]

Shaken and angered by the announcement of the marriage and the symbolic victory it connotes for Flem, Ratliff feels suffocated by the heat of "spent summer." The first thing he sees is the village store, emblem of Yoknapatawpha's ruin, then the blacksmith shop and the metal roof of the gin, both signs of the age of iron that has overtaken the land. The very air laden with the dust of processed cotton has been made to vibrate with a mechanical rhythm. Men seem to breathe the steam that powers the gin; cotton, once a plant of the fields, is here a product, to be processed or ground in the dust, subjugated like all of nature (the soot-stiffened weeds, or the mules and the men themselves) to the will and waste of the machine.

The scene becomes mythical without losing its specificity. It incarnates a psychic state, Ratliff's mood as he approaches the village. The persons involved in the situation and the situation itself expand into an image fusing their objective identity with Ratliff's sense of them. This involves no deletion or neglect of any level of meaning; on the contrary, the symbolic implications, even the mythical references Faulkner sees in a particular scene, seem to emerge clearly only when he also evokes the scene realistically. Thus when Ratliff, as narrator in one section of *The Hamlet*, offers this purple invocation of Eula: "her entire

[1] *The Hamlet*, p. 3.

appearance suggested some symbology out of the old Dionysic times—honey in sunlight and bursting grapes, the writhen bleeding of the crushed fecundated vine beneath the hard rapacious trampling goat-hoof'' (p. 164), we need an equally developed sense of Eula as the somewhat over-ripe daughter of a local farmer to see the point of the myth-ical allusion, which lies essentially in its wondrous incon-gruity.

This interplay between realism and mythical enlarge-ment which Faulkner needed to invoke those larger-than-life grotesques can be seen working in the most successful conjurings of the monstrous Flem. In one such moment, a group of Yoknapatawpha rustics express their wonder at Flem's inhuman silence. One of them allows as that Flem probably conceals his business even from his kinfolk. A local legend is created when a second man embroiders on this: "the first man Flem would tell his business to would be the man that was left after the last man died. Flem Snopes don't even tell himself what he is up to. Not if he was laying in bed with himself in a empty house in the dark of the moon" (p. 96).

For all its fantastic, imaginative element, the American tall tale depends also upon a profound realism, both to be told and to be understood. Faulkner's interest in the genre was already evident in *Mosquitoes* (1927) in a tale of sheep become swamp alligators. In *The Hamlet* it defines the kind of myth-making its author was best at: not in the mode of Spenser or Yeats but like that of Bret Harte and Mark Twain.[2] In the context in which they originated—an almost

---

[2] The extreme example of *The Fable* indicates that allegory was not Faulkner's forte. Nor was any form of abstraction, really; he was most at home within the complexities of the felt, lived moment, of unanalyzed

exclusively agrarian South—Sut Lovingood and Simon Suggs constituted Faulkner's kind of myth, that is, they functioned with relation to everyone's acquaintance with real "crackers." But in the New South episodes of the trilogy and in its general concern with the New South, the irredeemable redneck was out of context and faded into an abstraction vaguely signifying a lack of ethics and culture. In that setting the horrific Snopeses are sadly reduced. Without the perspective and the color lent by Faulkner's usually superabundant settings, the fabled Eula turns into a suburban matron, Gavin becomes embarrassing, his nephew takes to whining, and even Ratliff grows quaint. As for Flem, in *The Town*, the arch-subversive becomes a Tory. Exchanging his cap for a black felt hat, he disappears into the Establishment, slipping into the future as silently and without trace as he had appeared out of the past already an allegorical cipher.

One day there had been no Snopeses visible anywhere in the county. The next Jody Varner looked up in his father's store to see Ab Snopes "silhouetted by the open door . . . standing with a curious planted stiffness" (p. 8). There is something vaguely troubling about Ab's materialization, something which becomes ominous when Flem himself later enters the scene. Again it is Jody who sees him for the first time "suddenly in one of the sashless windows [of the Snopes cabin] and without knowing when it had come there, a face beneath a gray cloth cap, the lower jaw moving steadily and rhythmically which even as he shouted 'Hello!' vanished again." And reappeared: "one

and often even half-understood experience. The intellectual reduction and the separation into categories necessary to the allegory exclude just the textures and relationships Faulkner wrote best about.

moment the road had been empty, the next moment the man stood there beside it . . . the same cloth cap, the same rhythmically chewing jaw materialized apparently out of nothing and almost abreast of the horse, with an air of the completely and purely accidental which [Jody] Varner was to remember and speculate about only later" (pp. 22, 25).

A Snopes always emerges suddenly, unannounced and unexplained. This is paradoxically juxtaposed to the complete stability of the character once he has erupted onto the scene. The "planted stiffness" of Ab's first appearance, framed in the doorway as Flem's face is framed in the window, expresses the stasis of these self-contained entities, wrapped in neat rigid packages. Flem looks exactly the same the second time Jody sees him as he did the first, even to his rhythmic chewing, a characteristic instance of movement defining stasis.[3] A Snopes seems somehow able to move more rapidly than anyone can follow, yet he himself never changes. The discontinuity of "one moment . . . the next" explains how he does it: the process, the development that normally orders human lives is missing from his. Flem and the Snopeses proceed in their conquest by a series of discontinuous leaps, more or less frequent, shorter or longer, charting a course that can be traced only in retrospect.

But none of these qualities has a necessary source in the "real" character of the Snopeses; nothing in their origin or in their socioeconomic role could explain the peculiar way they enter the country. Rather, these qualities illus-

---

[3] Rhythmic movement generally conveys an ominous quality in Faulkner's writing. He seems to consider its mechanical, automatic aspect as the antithesis of the unpredictable and irregular dynamic of life.

trate the given allegorical meaning of Snopesism as a catastrophe, an invasion, perhaps a retribution for past sins. The futile defense waged by Ratliff, Gavin Stevens, and Charles Mallison, with its emphasis on keeping the Snopeses out, takes for granted the self-contained and non-historical character of the threat. None of the three seems to see Snopesism as a domestic development.

Chick: 'So when I say "we" and "we thought" what I mean is Jefferson and what Jefferson thought. . . .'
Stevens: 'So . . . they—when I say "they" I mean Snopeses'';

Gavin going off to war charges Ratliff:

'You'll have to hold the fort now. You'll have to tote the load . . . think you can hold them till I get back?'
Ratliff: 'Not me, nor a hundred of me . . . the only thing is to get shut of them, abolish them.'

Stevens' answer removes the Snopeses even further from human history by lending them mystical significance:

'No, no . . . no, we got them now; they're ourn now; I don't know just what Jefferson could a committed back there whenever it was, to have won this punishment, gained this right, earned this privilege. But we did. So it's for us to cope, to resist; us to endure and (if we can) survive.' [4]

Faulkner himself echoed this theme when he said that Snopes is "the old Adam in man . . . there is something in man that will always fight Snopes." [5] Stevens considers Snopes simply the embodiment of the rapacity that is in every man, thus neither the agent, the victim, nor the cre-

[4] *The Town*, pp. 3, 33, 102.   [5] *Faulkner in the University*, p. 34.

ator of social forces, but the force itself whose equivalent in *Absalom, Absalom!* is not Sutpen but slavery, or rather not even slavery but the pure evil embodied in it.[6]

While Sutpen and his representative career comprise the reality with which *Absalom, Absalom!* is concerned, Flem is only an embodied quality afloat from any particular situation. Thus, Flem's behavior even in the social realm can have no social pertinence. He does not even represent commercialism or the business ethic of the New South, and the admirable Wallstreet Panic Snopes demonstrates that storekeepers can be excellent people and still succeed. Faulkner once said that he had a high regard for Wall because he "wanted to be independent, wanted to make money but he had rules about how he was going to do it, he wanted to make money by simple industry, the old rules of working hard and saving your pennies, not by taking advantages of anybody."[7] Even Poor Richard would have approved. Wall's old-fashioned virtue proves so remunerative that he eventually builds Jefferson's first supermarket in partnership with Ratliff, who proudly attributes his partner's excellent credit rating to the fact that "he aint cutting into nobody's private business, he's helping all business." That Flem chooses to earn his money by other than "simple industry" then is apparently not to be blamed on any inherent features of the business world. Indeed Flem's unethical behavior does not seem even altogether functional. He does make unusually good profits selling dubious ham-

[6] Warren Beck in *Man in Motion, Faulkner's Trilogy* (Madison, Wis., 1961) views Snopes as an allegorical personification of evil, the representation of ubiquitous evil. However, Beck sees no thematic or artistic drawback to this allegorical method because he considers that Faulkner was generally concerned first with abstract, universal issues.

• [7] *Faulkner in the University*, p. 246.

burgers and later also does well on the brass fittings he steals from the Oxford electric generator. But all this seems peripheral to his eventual success. As a banker, in fact, he is entirely orthodox, as Gavin himself had predicted he would be: ". . . we expected no more of even a Snopes bank vice president than simple conformation to pattern."[8]

It is therefore not the bank (which, unlike the plantation in *Absalom, Absalom!,* appears to be morally neutral) with which Gavin does battle, nor Flem the banker, but Flem Snopes as allegorically abstract evil. But if Flem makes no real difference to the structure of Yoknapatawpha life, if he carries out the old policies in the old way, what makes him so bad? Gavin Stevens must have seen more to fear than lack of breeding and tobacco chewing, but one cannot tell what from *The Town.* Perhaps one reason Stevens has lost stature in this middle volume of the trilogy is that both he and Flem seem to lack motive and rationale, as the novel lacks substance. This points up a basic flaw in the allegorical treatment of the Snopeses, that in the end its abstraction undercuts even its own abstract morality. Without content the threat of Flem evaporates along with his literary presence.

Nor can the novel speak to its more general historical theme, for the South that bred Sartoris, Sutpen, and Joe Christmas is only passively and incidentally involved in the rise of Snopesism. The moral weakness that leaves Yoknapatawpha vulnerable to the Snopeses may be rooted in its history but Snopesism itself is not. Because Jason is a Compson, his mercenary attitudes, no less than Quentin's morbidity, must be seen as somehow relevant to the aristo-

[8] *The Town,* pp. 150, 137.

cratic South. But Flem is no kin at all to the people he dis-
possesses and his victory over them exposes only their
weakness. It is true that the Snopeses are old Southerners,
but only in the sense that they have been around a long
time: their long presence in the region constitutes duration
rather than history for they have remained what they
always were, a constant threat to Southern civilization
somewhat like the plague or a foreign invasion whose hor-
ror is a function of its alien quality; whereas the fear Sutpen inspired in Quentin Compson and in other Southern
aristocrats sprang from their recognition in him of themselves. Indeed the formal aspects of the Snopes saga indicate that when Faulkner approached the subject of the
modern South, [9] he turned away from exploratory, open-
ended forms—such as the recalling plot. And now that he
sought to dramatize rather than to discover, the allegory
became newly congenial to him—though, as I have suggested before, only conceptually, and not temperamentally
nor through the natural tendencies of his talent.

Faulkner himself was not at all pleased with *The Town*
and complained that when he moved to Jefferson, Snopes
"let me down." He was no longer even "a good first-rate
scoundrel." [10] He probably realized too that the modern
setting of *The Town* was partly at fault, for he began the
third and last volume of the saga not only back in rural
Yoknapatawpha but among old agrarian issues he had not
raised even in *The Hamlet*. Instead of Will Varner, who, as
we saw, popularized the cavalier image, the central land-

---

[9] It may be too that the fact that *The Town* was written relatively late
in Faulkner's career contributes to its diminished vitality.

[10] *Faulkner in the University*, pp. 32–33. (Session of March 7, 1957.)

owner in the first episode of *The Mansion* is Jack Houston, a much less accessible gentleman who raises thoroughbred horses. The story of Houston's tragic life and death is told in all three of the Snopes novels, but with a different stress corresponding closely to the ideological character of each. In *The Hamlet*, which is especially bemused with the oddities of the Mississippi countryside and the peculiar aberrations it seems to breed (this being where the famous story of Isaac Snopes's idyll with his cow appears), we read primarily of Houston's obsessional relationship with his wife and of her gothic death beneath the hooves of Houston's prize stallion. *The Town* has little concern with such country matters and mentions them only in passing, but *The Mansion* begins with an elaborate and newly sociological version which focuses on Houston's fatal encounter with Mink Snopes. The revived class character of the cavalier which Houston connotes is matched by Mink's replacement of Flem as the focal redneck. For Mink, although a cousin of Flem, emerges from Sutpen's world through a typological development that is at odds with the assumptions of the Snopes construct.

His character goes all the way back to one of the first pieces Faulkner wrote during his New Orleans period, a sketch called "The Hill" (1922). In it a nameless "tieless casual" is described climbing a hill to stand for a few moments looking about over the squalid village to which he presently returns. The episode is without a plot as the man is virtually without identity. At the end we return to the beginning; but in between there has been the most tentative of developments in a direction which would be an increasingly fruitful one for Faulkner to pursue. The man is a migrant worker who has just finished a "day of harsh labor with his hands, a strife against the forces of nature to gain bread and clothing and a place to sleep." "In this way," Faulkner explains, "he worked out the devastating unimportance of his destiny, with a mind heretofore untroubled by moral quibbles and principles." Now, for a brief instant, this barely-human being has been "shaken at last by the faint resistless force of spring in a valley at sunset." [11] His feelings never rise fully to consciousness and they sink with the sun, but they forecast clearly two major themes in Faulkner's fiction: the submerged humanity of the inarticulate and the inspiration to a higher consciousness inherent in nature.

Indeed the sketch is remarkable for thus early naming a number of the ideas the author later elaborated. There is, for example, a suggestive paradox in the situation of a man dulled by combat with nature who is also enlivened by her, something which Faulkner would explore in the career of Mink which we are now discussing. It is also apparent, of course, that he was at this point only beginning to define his concerns which are here generalized and unfocused. Thus the man appears to represent all of mankind, "a world of endless toil and troubled slumber," as it wrests its miserable keep from vaguely defined "forces of nature." The social element in this struggle is completely missing although it would play a major role in later treatments. But the formal problem which primarily limits the quality of the sketch and the philosophical issue it raises are the same ones I focused on in analyzing works like "The Spotted Horses" and "The Horseswap" written at the other end of

[11] "The Hill," rpt. in *William Faulkner, Early Prose and Poetry,* ed. Carvel Collins (Boston, 1962), pp. 91–92.

Faulkner's career: the kind and degree of consciousness in lower-class characters.

For the inability of the protagonist to think or speak for himself essentially prevents his quickening, while the sketch as a whole falls prey to its narrative voice murmuring about "nymphs and fauns" who "riot to a shrilling of pipes, to a shivering and hissing of cymbals in a sharp volcanic abasement beneath a tall icy star." Thus "The Hill" also represents Faulkner's first use of the frame device; Gavin Stevens must have just returned from Heidelberg.

At a later stage of the development toward Mink Snopes, Stevens narrates the story of Monk, "a moron, perhaps even a cretin," an inmate at the state penitentiary who murders the warden and is executed. As district attorney and student of human nature, Stevens wants to know why Monk has killed a man he loved: at the time of the killing Monk was knitting his victim a sweater which he races to finish before his own death. He is thus not much more mentally competent than the man on the hill with whom he shares a desultory background. Born in the pine hill country, he knows only how to make whiskey and handle a shotgun and his body is no better than his mind. Yet something stirs in him which he finally articulates standing with the black hood already over his head, waiting to be hanged. "Now," he says distinctly, "I am going out into the free world, and farm." Monk's puzzling last words lead Stevens to investigate and discover that he had first heard them from a fellow prisoner who instigated the warden's murder by telling Monk that

'here we all were, pore ignorant country folks that hadn't had no chance. That God had made to live outdoors in the free world and farm his land for Him; only we were pore and ignorant and didn't know it, and the rich folks wouldn't tell us until it was too late. That we were pore ignorant country folks that never saw a train before, getting on the train and nobody caring to tell us where to get off and farm in the free world like God wanted us to do.'

This argument had moved Monk deeply, in Faulkner's words "establishing at last that contact with the old, fecund, ponderable travailing earth which he wanted but had not been able to tell about." [12]

And he still wasn't telling it, since it not only takes Gavin Stevens to explain to us what he meant, but also the demagogic prisoner to tell him what to say. That the prisoner is a demagogue constitutes one of the layers of qualification wrapped about Monk's socially threatening statement which is furthermore structurally contained in a frame within a frame: the prisoner tells Gavin, who, on what is really still a third framing level, tells his nephew, Charles Mallison, who, not surprisingly, doubts the whole story and advises us that it would be incomprehensible if in recreating it he had not used "the nebulous tools of supposition and inference and invention." Thus the whole thing becomes a literary exercise whose content need not trouble us. Should the story still evoke sympathy, it is further undercut by Mallison's assurance that Monk "could not have wanted [to farm] before, or he would have, since he could have found chances enough." [13] But the story otherwise pities Monk for being inarticulate even with him-

[12] William Faulkner, "Monk," *Knight's Gambit* (New York, 1956), pp. 38, 44, 35.
[13] "Monk," p. 35.

self and makes this a key aspect of his victimization, so that Mallison's reassurance would seem beside the point.

In fact, this lack of accord between two levels of the same work points to the tension between them and within Faulkner's attitude to the subject. This tension arises from the strong appeal of the prisoner's words despite their dishonest intent. In short, they appeal to Faulkner as they do to Monk, because they evoke the powerful image of a simple man tilling the soil of God's good earth. But for that image to unfold in the context of the Yoknapatawpha social structure, it would eventually have to challenge Gavin Stevens himself and the narration he shares with his nephew—the situation is already familiar from the discussion of the framed tale of Southwestern humor: the form and content of the story develop toward an annihilative confrontation.

Putting the subversive ideas into the mouth of a demagogue, however, expresses Faulkner's ambivalence in a relatively stable form. Demagogy is, after all, the exploitation of ambiguity, so that this would seem a minor instance of the sort represented by Sutpen, a fictional situation which thrives on the author's uncertainty. It doesn't work here for a somewhat complicated reason. The story starts out to discover why Monk killed the warden but it ends up only telling us how he came to do it. As far as it develops its initial purpose, it seems to suggest that Monk murdered the only person he loved because in the depths of his deprivation the most creative impulses had become fatally destructive. How he came to commit the crime is more readily explained by the plot of a conniving man with a grudge against the warden and a gullible half-wit. I think that

Faulkner shifted to the latter, much less interesting version, because he was unwilling for the moment to confront the genuine appeal in the demagogue's spiel. He focused instead on the evil of demagogy regardless of its material, thus essentially begging the question he had started out to explore.

As it happened, moreover, the story's new subject serves to entrench the Gavin Stevens point of view more firmly than ever. The opportunism of the prison inmate is overshadowed by that of the state's governor, who refuses Stevens' request that he avenge Monk by denying parole to his tormentor, because the politician wants no unpleasantness in an election year. As narrator, Charles Mallison explains that the governor was "a man without ancestry and with but little more divulged background than Monk had." With his advent the forces of the story are thus confused beyond unraveling. This effigy of Vardaman or Bilbo enlists no supporters when he accuses Stevens of "trying to bring the notions of 1860 into the politics of the nineteen hundreds." At that point we may be a little vague about which aspects of the cavalier code might work to a cracker's advantage, but we certainly want none of these new modern politics. The governor indeed is not trying to win us over; the only attractive thing about him is that he pretends neither to a higher purpose nor a better class. "You are what my grandpap would have called a gentleman," he tells Stevens. "He would have snarled it at you, hating you and your kind; he might very well have shot your horse from under you someday from behind a fence—for a principle." [14] Mink Snopes does better: he

[14] "Monk," p. 41. The governor is thus a prototype of the neo-populists Vardaman and Bilbo whose careers as governors of Mississippi

shoots the gentleman himself—for the principle of agrarian equality.

The first significant aspect of the story of Mink Snopes is that it is told from his own point of view. And, as he sees it, the fatal dispute began "at the very instant Houston was born already shaped for arrogance and intolerance and pride." [15] Its final stage begins the morning Houston nearly rode down Mink and cursed him afterward, demanding "Why in hell didn't you jump when you heard me coming?" Mink broods over the incident and the way Houston "thund [ers] up and down the road" "until a fellow that never had anything but his own two legs to travel on, would have to jump clean off the road into the bushes or the son-of-a-bitching horse would have killed him too with its shod feet and left him there in the ditch for the son-of-a-bitching hound to eat before Houston would even have reported it" (p. 11). Then he ambushes Houston and shoots him right off his horse. The conflict between the planter and the redneck is at this point completely polarized with the participants sharply delineated as the very types of their class. No other aristocrat in the county besides Houston is identified by such quasi-medieval emblems as a blooded stallion and a "hound," and Mink is as carefully dressed for his part "in the slicker held together with baling wire and automobile tire patching which was the only winter outergarment he owned over his worn patched overalls" (pp. 11–12).

The social basis of their quarrel is similarly clear and undiluted, for Mink does not kill Houston merely out of

---

are described and analyzed by Albert D. Kirwan in *Revolt of the Rednecks: Mississippi Politics: 1876–1925.*

[15] *The Mansion*, p. 7.

abstract principle. He has tangible cause for his hatred in an incident featuring Mink's one emaciated cow and Houston's vast holdings, an alignment of forces whose rhetorical intent is inescapable. The half-starved cow wanders into Houston's lush pasture one fall day, and Mink decides to leave her there to winter with the planter's herd. When Houston discovers this, he invites Snopes to "come and get that bonerack of yours" out of his feed lot but Snopes ignores the request. Every afternoon that winter Mink goes up the road "to watch Houston's pedigreed beef herd, his own sorry animal among them, move, not even hurrying into the barn which was warmer and tighter against the weather than the cabin he lived in . . . cursing the rich feed devoted to cattle instead of humans . . . cursing above all the unaware white man through or because of whose wealth such a condition could obtain" (pp. 11–12).

In the spring Houston refuses to return the cow pending payment of eight dollars for her fodder, and Mink has to work out the amount. At this point he has not yet determined to kill the planter; that decision comes when, at the conclusion of the allotted labors, Houston demands one dollar more for the extra time he has fed the cow while Mink settled his debt.

Mink works out the added sum. He shouts to Houston over the roar of the shotgun, "I ain't shooting you because of them thirty-seven and a half four-bit days . . . I killed you because of that-ere extry one-dollar pound fee" (p. 39). Thus presented, Houston's demand does seem excessive and Mink justified in seeing the whole thing in class terms. When the redneck appeals the additional fee to the unofficial local arbitrator, appropriately enough, Will Varner, the latter denies Mink's challenge because he is "afraid, afraid for the peace and quiet of the community which he held in his iron usurious hand, buttressed by the mortgages and liens in the vast iron safe in his store." (p. 19). Mink explains it all very clearly in his apostrophe to the murdered Houston: "Likely Will Varner couldn't do nothing else, being a rich man too and all you rich folks has got to stick together or else maybe someday the ones that aint rich might take a notion to raise up and take hit away from you" (p. 39). This culminates the development begun so tentatively in "The Hill" of a necessarily self-defining, lower-class consciousness.

So powerfully did Faulkner evoke this consciousness, which drew vitality also from the author's abstract sympathy with its basic democratic agrarian tenets, that when the others (Gavin Stevens, his nephew, and Ratliff) had failed, he turned to Mink, the neo-yeoman, as a last hope against impending doom.[16] And it would seem that Mink succeeds since *The Mansion* closes with his execution of Flem and thus presumably the end of Snopesism. But Faulkner's faith in the Minks of Yoknapatawpha came too late both in their lives and in his, for Mink, like Monk, realizes his full identity only at the moment of death, thus releasing Faulkner also from the consequences and implications of a redneck triumph.

As Faulkner explicitly links the two incidents, Mink goes into battle with Flem wearing all the decorations he has earned fighting Houston. Mink had expected Flem to arrange his defense when he was arrested for shooting the planter. He had counted on the solidarity of his kind, but instead Flem acquiesced gladly when Mink was given a life

[16] Gavin Stevens, Charles Mallison, and Ratliff presumably share this hope since they connive at the release of Mink Snopes from prison.

sentence. Thirty-eight years later Mink is paroled and goes straight to Jefferson to exact vengeance from the renegade. Thus the tradition and family-oriented Southern values that Flem's Snopesism betrays after such as Jason Compson and Thomas Sutpen had also betrayed them, now assume their final shape in the tribal but also class credo of a sharecropper. Still, this represents less of a commitment on Faulkner's part than it might appear because Mink, despite his outburst against Houston nearly forty years earlier, is so weak that to champion his cause is rather more sentimental than subversive. The close ties to the soil, which so invigorated Jefferson's yeoman, have totally debilitated Mink Snopes, as they had the man on the hill and Monk. " 'You got me,' " he admits, speaking to the land beneath his feet:

. . . you'll wear me out because you are stronger than me since I'm jest bone and flesh. I can't leave you because I can't afford to, and you know it. Me and what used to be the passion and excitement of my youth until you wore out the youth and I forgot the passion, will be here next year with the children of our passion for you to wear that much nearer the grave, and you know it; and the year after that, and the year after that, and you know that too. And not just me, but all my tenant and cropper kind that have immolated youth and hope on thirty or forty or fifty acres of dirt that wouldn't nobody but our kind work because you're all our kind have. (pp. 90–91)

There is cause enough for Mink's despair in the real conditions of Southern farming and, nationally, in the plight of the lone farmer amidst vast agro-factories. But the hopelessness of Mink's situation functions on another level as well, to disarm Faulkner into expressing the " 'cropper' " point of view without the disclaimer of a narrative frame or other device. Another way of saying this may be that the author could (in the literary sense) imagine the South egalitarian only at the point of its general disintegration. Thus the graveyard realizes Mink's dream of equality among his fellow agrarians. Deep in the earth, he thinks, "folks are all mixed and jumbled up comfortable and easy so wouldn't nobody know or even care who was which any more, himself among them, equal to any, good as any, brave as any, being inextricable from, anonymous with all of them: the beautiful, the splendid, the proud and the brave. . . ." A dying Mink becomes only abstractly and therefore unproblematically agrarian. Crowning the lowliness of Mink's harsh life with the exalted apotheosis of his death seems on the surface to resolve Faulkner's ambivalence. With Mink, he may have wanted to rise at last to their common agrarian ideal (above Yoknapatawpha's contending ideologies).

But the final encounter between Flem and Mink reveals the opposing camps still held and no treaty in sight. As characters, Mink and Flem are defined in different fictive universes. Flem emerges from the humorist tradition to express Faulkner's aristocratic fears, while he constructs Mink out of an opposite impulse toward a kind of critical realism or, at any rate, a critique of conventional attitudes. The two meet head-on and since neither has been able to win a decisive victory in Faulkner's mind, they destroy one another, cancel each other out really, without achieving a resolution. Thus, at the end, *The Mansion* just disintegrates. Flem's defeat, which has been the central motive for the entire trilogy, is now accomplished without any consequences whatsoever. It means nothing. Ratliff has learned that "there aren't any morals, people just do the best they can . . . the pore sons of bitches." Stevens is old and tired, and, astonishingly, he declines to explain. Flem dead, Mink sinks "down and down into the ground" to rise "equal to any . . . anonymous with all of them . . . among the shining phantoms and dreams which are the milestones of the long human recording" (pp. 435, 436), the recording that is now ended.

Index